1,000,000 Books

are available to read at

Forgotten Books

www.ForgottenBooks.com

Read online
Download PDF
Purchase in print

ISBN 978-1-330-13016-2
PIBN 10033153

This book is a reproduction of an important historical work. Forgotten Books uses state-of-the-art technology to digitally reconstruct the work, preserving the original format whilst repairing imperfections present in the aged copy. In rare cases, an imperfection in the original, such as a blemish or missing page, may be replicated in our edition. We do, however, repair the vast majority of imperfections successfully; any imperfections that remain are intentionally left to preserve the state of such historical works.

Forgotten Books is a registered trademark of FB &c Ltd.
Copyright © 2018 FB &c Ltd.
FB &c Ltd, Dalton House, 60 Windsor Avenue, London, SW19 2RR.
Company number 08720141. Registered in England and Wales.

For support please visit www.forgottenbooks.com

1 MONTH OF FREE READING

at

www.ForgottenBooks.com

By purchasing this book you are eligible for one month membership to ForgottenBooks.com, giving you unlimited access to our entire collection of over 1,000,000 titles via our web site and mobile apps.

To claim your free month visit:

www.forgottenbooks.com/free33153

* Offer is valid for 45 days from date of purchase. Terms and conditions apply.

English
Français
Deutsche
Italiano
Español
Português

www.forgottenbooks.com

Mythology Photography **Fiction** Fishing Christianity **Art** Cooking Essays Buddhism Freemasonry Medicine **Biology** Music **Ancient Egypt** Evolution Carpentry Physics Dance Geology **Mathematics** Fitness Shakespeare **Folklore** Yoga Marketing **Confidence** Immortality Biographies Poetry **Psychology** Witchcraft Electronics Chemistry History **Law** Accounting **Philosophy** Anthropology Alchemy Drama Quantum Mechanics Atheism Sexual Health **Ancient History Entrepreneurship** Languages Sport Paleontology Needlework Islam **Metaphysics** Investment Archaeology Parenting Statistics Criminology **Motivational**

PLAY-HOUSE OF A GARDENER BOWER-BIRD

These birds (*Amblyornis subalaris*) construct a beautiful domed hut around a small tree or shrub, which they interlace with twigs. At the foot of the tree, inside the hut, they build up a bank of moss and decorate it with flowers. In this pretty pavilion they spend many hours at play.

THE WONDERS
OF
BIRD LIFE

STING ACCOUNT OF THE EDUCATION, COURTSHIP,
PLAY, ELOPEMENTS, FIGHTING & OTHER
ACTIONS IN THE LIFE OF BIRDS

BY

JOHN LEA, M.A.

JOINT AUTHOR OF
"ANIMAL ARTS AND CRAFTS," &c. &c.

WITH EIGHT ILLUSTRATIONS

PHILADELPHIA
B. LIPPINCOTT COMPANY
LONDON: SEELEY, SERVICE & CO. LTD.

PLAY HOUSE OF A GARDENER BOWER-BIRD

These birds (*Amblyornis subalaris*) construct a beautiful domed hut around a small tree or shrub, which they interlace with twigs. At the foot of the tree, inside the hut, they build up a lawn of moss and decorate it with flowers. In this pretty pavilion they spend many hours at play.

THE WONDERS
OF
BIRD LIFE

AN INTERESTING ACCOUNT OF THE EDUCATION, COURTSHIP,
SPORT & PLAY, MAKEBELIEVE, FIGHTING & OTHER
ASPECTS OF THE LIFE OF BIRDS

BY

JOHN LEA, M.A.

JOINT AUTHOR OF
"THE ROMANCE OF ANIMAL ARTS AND CRAFTS," &c. &c.

WITH EIGHT ILLUSTRATIONS

PHILADELPHIA
J. B. LIPPINCOTT COMPANY
LONDON: SEELEY, SERVICE & CO. LTD.
1912

CONTENTS

CHAPTER I

NURSERY DAYS AND EDUCATION

The hatching of a chick—How the egg-shell is cracked—The 'egg-tooth' and its uses—Different ways of escape from the shell—Helplessness and precocity: Parrot and Partridge—Instinct—How to distinguish instinctive actions—Life within the egg—Obedience of the unborn chick—Chicken language—Fearlessness of young birds—Playing 'possum—Protective colouration—Early feats of skill—Learning to peck—Food and experience—Learning to drink :—The flight instinct—Parental discipline—Swimming and diving—Young water-birds which are launched by their parents—Protection of nestlings—Learning to sing—Nest-building—Nests and eggs—Early misdeeds: Cuckoos and their victims—Instinct and education 17

CHAPTER II

SITTING

Incubation period — Division of labour — Domesticated husbands — Swifts—A rebellious hen—The cloistered Hornbill—Manner of leaving and returning to the nest—Protective colouration—Scene in a heronry—Pelican Island—Incubation under difficulties—Cold and heat 35

CHAPTER III

BIRDS' INCUBATORS

Extremes of the brooding instinct—Aids to incubation—Sun-warmth: its advantages and dangers—Ostrich, Sand-Grouse, and Black-backed Courser—The Mound-Builders and their incubators—Maleos—Choice of ground—Hot springs—The buried chick—Brush-Turkey—Heat from fermenting vegetable matter—Attending to the incubator—Large feet of Mound-birds—Megapodes—Immense size of mounds—Ocellated Megapode—Precocity of Mound-bird chicks—Volcanic heat 49

CONTENTS

CHAPTER IV

FEEDING THE CHICKS

Infant-food and why it is necessary—Finches—Change of diet and special preparation of food—'Pigeon's milk'—Insect-eaters—Swallows and Swifts—A ball of flies—Reed-Warblers—Industry of parents—A working day of sixteen hours—Feeding the young in mid-air—Methods of giving food—An interesting experiment—Birds-of-Prey—Larders—Fish-eaters—Fish soup—Perverted instinct of domesticated birds 67

CHAPTER V

DEFENCE OF HOME AND FAMILY

Change of character in breeding season—Courage and endurance—Braving cold, water, fire, famine, etc.—Intimidation—Strategy: the wiles of a Woodchuck—Attitude of an angry bird—Animals attacked by nesting birds: cats, dogs, pigs—Birds-of-Prey—Courage of Owls—The redoubtable King-bird—'Bonxies' and bonneting—An unpleasant habit—One of nature's comedians . . . 80

CHAPTER VI

MAKE-BELIEVE: A STUDY IN INSTINCT

Deceptive behaviour—The 'little brown bird'—Death-feigning—Lapwings and egg-gatherers—Wiles of the male bird and protective colouration of the eggs—Avosets and Stilts—Ducks and Drakes—Ostrich—Unkingly conduct of a King Vulture—Some artful dodgers—A cat's hunting—The paralysing effect of fear, and the advantage which hunters take of it—Difference between death-feigning and the immobility of protectively coloured birds—The real 'possum—The popular idea of a 'shamming' bird—A true fairy-tale—Natural selection 94

CHAPTER VII

SPORT AND PLAY

The meaning and importance of play—Fighting games—Playful pecking of tame birds—Nursing and nest-building play—Flying games—Swimming games—'Follow-my-leader'—Hide-and-seek of climbing birds—Swinging—Birds and children—Toys and playthings—Mischief and destructiveness—Practical jokes . . 111

CONTENTS

CHAPTER VIII

PLAYGROUNDS AND PAVILIONS

The Paradise-bird's playing-tree—Beauty on a pedestal—The Argus Pheasant's drawing-room—A wonderful courtship display—Sexual selection—The Polyplectron's playground and courtship—The club-grounds of Game-birds—Bower-birds and their pleasure-houses—Satin Bower-birds at the 'Zoo'—Decorating the bower—A dêpot for lost property—Courtship-play—The Spotted Bower-bird's avenue and playthings—The Regent Bower-bird's love of colour—Carpeted playgrounds—The Gardener-birds and their beautiful pleasure-grounds—The Golden Bower-bird's toy village and triumphal arch   124

CHAPTER IX

COURTSHIP

Excess of bachelors amongst birds, and its results—Arts of peace—Singing for a mate—The meaning of song—Song and dance—Instrumental music—The drumming of Snipes—Courtship flights—The dalliance of Eagles—Antics of Game-birds—The indifference of hens—Bustards in Spain—Coyness and provocation—Feminine boldness: the Northern Phalarope—Good-humoured rivalry: the Flickers   143

THE contents of this book have been taken from Mr. John Lea's larger book entitled "The Romance of Bird Life," published at five shillings.

LIST OF ILLUSTRATIONS

	PAGE
PLAYHOUSE OF A GARDENER BOWER-BIRD	*Frontispiece*
OSTRICH CHICK LEAVING THE EGG	24
BROWN PELICANS ON PELICAN ISLAND	44
DEVOTED PARENTS: REED-WARBLERS AND NEST	72
THE BUTCHER-BIRD'S LARDER	76
DEFENDING THE NEST: GANDER ATTACKING A SOW	88
LAPWING LEAVING ITS NEST	98
WHITE STORK AND HIS PLAYMATES	120

THE WONDERS OF
BIRD LIFE

BIRD LIFE

CHAPTER I

NURSERY DAYS AND EDUCATION

The hatching of a chick—How the egg-shell is cracked—The 'egg-tooth' and its uses—Different ways of escape from the shell—Helplessness and precocity: Parrot and Partridge—Instinct—How to distinguish instinctive actions—Life within the egg—Obedience of the unborn chick—Chicken language—Fearlessness of young birds—Playing 'possum—Protective colouration—Early feats of skill—Learning to peck—Food and experience—Learning to drink—The flight instinct—Parental discipline—Swimming and diving—Young water-birds which are launched by their parents—Protection of nestlings—Learning to sing—Nest-building—Nests and eggs—Early misdeeds: Cuckoos and their victims—Instinct and education.

NOWHERE in the wide range of animal life is there a greater wealth and variety of romance than amongst birds. In their loves, their battles, their adventures, in all their varied activities and social habits, there is present that curiously pervading charm which constitutes, for those who have not had the misfortune to become deaf to its appeal, the very true spirit of romance. Nor is the element of mystery, which is so often bound up with romance, wholly wanting, for there is still much in the life of a bird that we cannot explain or understand, in spite of the great progress which science has made towards the far-off goal of complete knowledge.

NURSERY DAYS AND EDUCATION

Before we reach the end of our story we shall have occasion to make the acquaintance of birds of many kinds, some of them, it may be, but little known even to naturalists; but we will bear in mind that interesting birds are not necessarily rare, and that there is abundance of romance in the life of species with which we are all quite familiar—so familiar, perhaps, that many people never take the trouble really to observe them at all. For the moment we need not go far afield—no further than to the fowl-pen.

The interest of a bird's life story begins with the very earliest days while the chick is still in the egg, unborn, and there is no reason why we should not take that as our starting-point; indeed, if we do so, we shall meet at once with some of the most remarkable and beautiful instances of the way in which Nature has made provision for carrying on her work of aiding and safeguarding the appearance on the earth of a new living creature.

What could be more commonplace than the hatching of an ordinary domestic chick? For three weeks or so the Hen broods over her eggs, and then one day she appears with a family of fluffy, cheeping youngsters about her, over which she fusses inordinately until they are able to look after themselves. If all goes well, they are, in due course, ready for the table, or to have nests of their own; and there very often the interest of their owner ends. Let us, however, watch the hatching of a chick and see if we cannot find out about it something more that is worth knowing. It is not possible, of course, to do this in ordinary circumstances, that is to say, while the egg is covered by a sitting Hen; we must either wait until several of the brood have escaped from the shell, when it is likely that the others are on the point of emerging, and remove one of the unhatched eggs to a warm place, such as a basket in front of the fire, where we can observe it conveniently; or, what is far better, watch eggs which are being hatched in an artificial glass-covered incubator. In either case a great deal of patience

NURSERY DAYS AND EDUCATION

may be called for, but we are not likely ever to learn very much about the ways of birds without that.

Let us suppose, then, that the eggs are hatching, and that we fix our attention on one which has still an unbroken shell. If we have been fortunate in our choice we shall probably see the egg moving a little from time to time, and if we listen intently we may hear a feeble tapping, caused by the chick hammering upon its prison walls in its efforts to escape. The sounds are not continuous; there are frequent pauses, some of them quite long, so we may suppose that the little prisoner finds its task a tiring one, and is obliged to rest from time to time. After a while, however, there appears in the shell a crack which grows gradually larger, until at length a piece is pushed right out, or the shell is broken quite in halves, and the chick is visible. It presents a rather pathetic, woebegone appearance, for its downy covering is bedraggled with moisture. Now and then it moves in a jerky way, opens its eyes, and makes heroic efforts to hold up its head, but it is not very successful in its attempts, for the eyes keep closing again, while the head slowly sinks to the floor. The little bird, indeed, seems to be in the last stage of exhaustion.

Gradually, however, the chick gathers strength, its downfeathers become dry, it practises raising itself on its feet, and it is not very long before it has learnt to stand up. Looking at it now, it appears much larger than it did just at first, and one is disposed to marvel that it could so recently have been shut up in such a narrow space. Certainly it had not very much room in which to move about, and its hammering on the hard shell must have been performed at a considerable disadvantage. It seems rather wonderful that it should have managed to escape at all: but perhaps the little beak is very hard and sharp? No, it is still quite soft; but if you look at it closely you will see at the very tip of the upper half of the bill a pale spot, and there is the instrument which Nature has provided to enable the chick to gain its freedom. It is a tiny

NURSERY DAYS AND EDUCATION

conical nodule of chalky substance, which is formed as the time for hatching approaches, and is known as the 'bill-scale' or 'egg-tooth.' As the chick moves its head about this instrument acts as a file, and gradually scrapes and weakens the shell where it rubs against it; then, when the time for more active measures arrives, it makes the feeble blows which the little bird delivers on the wall of its narrow prison far more effective than they would be if struck by a soft bill without any such armature. The 'egg-tooth' has no other use: when once the chick has emerged its work is done, and it soon disappears.

We ought, perhaps, to mention that the shell is not broken open in just the same way by all the different kinds of birds, for while many, like the domestic chick, gather sufficient strength after chipping a hole and breathing the air for a little while to burst open their prison walls, others, such as Ducks, chip the shell in a circle near the broad end, or, like the Humming-birds, make a clean, smooth cut round four-fifths of the equator before hooking their claws over the edge and pushing the two halves apart.

The domestic chick, then, is clothed when born in a coat of down; its eyes are open, and it is very soon able to stand on its feet: what else it can do we shall learn presently. The young of many birds, such as those of Gulls, Ducks, Plovers, Cranes, Ostriches, and so on, are equally advanced, and some of them are even more precocious.

But the young of another great group of birds, among which are Parrots, Hawks, Herons, Doves, Gannets, Crows, and all our song-birds, are more or less helpless when hatched, and many (though not all) of them are blind and naked. Being unable to leave the nest or to look after themselves in any way, they are entirely dependent on their parents for food and even, in the early days, for warmth.

When we come to inquire into the matter more closely, we find that the most highly developed and intelligent birds are

NURSERY DAYS AND EDUCATION

the most helpless at birth. A baby Parrot, for example, is unable to open its eyes for a week or more after escaping from the egg, and cannot leave the nest for at least thirty days—in the case of some of the larger Parrots it may be seven weeks. Even when it has learnt to fly it is still lovingly tended by its parents, and for some time longer is fed only on seeds which they have softened for it in their crops. What a contrast is this to the precocity of a young Sandpiper, which is able to run about almost as soon as it is born, and after an hour or two can cover the ground at an astonishing pace; or of a Partridge chick, which can jump over an obstacle four times its own height when only two or three days old!

The first thing which chicks endeavour to do is to discover a snug place where they can nestle close for warmth. In nature the little birds find this under their mother's wing, and in the incubator they huddle together; but in all circumstances they instinctively seek warmth, and they soon learn by experience where it is to be found, for hand-reared chickens will run to the hand of the person who tends them, and cosily ensconce themselves there, settling down in contentment and poking out their little heads between the fingers.

This brings us to one of the most interesting questions in bird-life: How far is a young bird guided by instinct, and to what extent are its actions due to experience and education? We cannot discuss it very fully here, for it is a difficult and complicated question, and one concerning which we have still a great deal to learn, although whole volumes have been written about it. I hope that some day you will read some of these books, especially those about *Animal Behaviour* and *Habit and Instinct*, by Professor Lloyd Morgan, which are more fascinating than any story-book. For the present we must be content with quite a short account of the matter.

We may say at once that birds are guided in their actions by both instinct and intelligence, but that with them instinct is the more highly developed of the two, while in man the exact

NURSERY DAYS AND EDUCATION

opposite is the case. A simple and fairly safe way of deciding whether what an animal does is the result of instinct or of intelligence is to inquire whether, in the same circumstances, it is done in the same or nearly the same way by all the individuals of the same species, age, and sex, without any previous experience to guide them. If so, the action is almost certainly the result of instinct, because there is a want of variety about actions which are truly instinctive which is very different from what we find in the case of rational actions. If you have ever kept silkworms you know that when the caterpillar has eaten a certain quantity of lettuce or mulberry leaves, it crawls into a corner and begins to spin a cocoon. There seems to be no particular reason why it should want to do anything of the kind; its surroundings are just the same as ever; it has the run of the same cardboard box, in the same exhilarating air of a school locker, with the same liberal supply of rather limp lettuce leaves; yet it appears suddenly to have tired of its sybaritic existence, and to be moved by some impulse from within to start spinning. That act is truly instinctive. There are other instinctive acts, however, which are not performed until some change takes place in the conditions to which the animal is exposed. Let us this time take the case of a bird by way of example. If you place a young Duckling, not very long out of the shell, in a pan of water, you can see it begin to paddle with its little legs and swim about on the top: that is an instinctive act brought about by exposing the bird to new conditions, or following, as we say, an external stimulus.

Most instinctive acts are either vitally important for the welfare of the race, like the silkworm's cocoon-spinning, which provides it with a cosy garment to protect it while it is in the helpless chrysalis condition; or, like the Duckling's swimming, they follow some external stimulus of frequent occurrence.

Chickens may often be heard cheeping while they are still in the shell, in some cases quite a long while before hatching. Ducklings begin their musical career about a day before they

NURSERY DAYS AND EDUCATION

make their appearance in the world, and young Moorhens as much as two days. The sound is sometimes quite spontaneous, but a silent eggling can often be induced to chirp in answer to a whistle. Now it has been noticed in more than one instance that if the mother utters a note of warning while the little prisoner is hammering away at the shell and singing (or is it complaining?) over its work, the sounds stop instantly, and the chick keeps quite still for a long time unless the old bird utters a different call which evidently means that the danger is past. That teaches us that the simple language of call-notes is certainly instinctive, for the chick within the egg cannot possibly have learnt their meaning by experience. Domestic chicks have at least six different call-notes, all expressing different meanings: a gentle piping of contentment, a low double note of enjoyment heard when the little bird is caressed, a cheep of discontent when it wants food or company, a squeak of protest when it is handled against its inclination, a shrill cry of distress when it is taken away from its companions, and, lastly, the peculiar danger cry. The danger cry seems to be a universal language, for it is understood by young birds of other species.

It is very important indeed that young birds should understand the parents' danger signals, because they seem to have no instinctive fear of any animal which approaches them quietly. If you are very gentle in your movements, you may feed nestlings without their showing signs of alarm unless their parents are present to utter a note of warning; and most people who have a cat and a garden are aware how frequently pussy is allowed by young birds to approach dangerously near, in her quiet, stealthy way, with fatal results. As for dogs, Professor Lloyd Morgan gives a most amusing instance of the natural absence of fear of them amongst young birds, in the case of his fox-terrier, which had been trained to be on his best behaviour and always to remain perfectly calm in the presence of chicks. As a result of his self-restraint the dog was treated with the utmost familiarity by all sorts of young birds: a Wild Duck

NURSERY DAYS AND EDUCATION

nibbled his lips; Plovers, Pheasants, and Partridges pecked his nose; and an ordinary chicken two and a half days old crept in under his body, and finding it nice and warm, cuddled down there! Now, if the parents of any of these little birds had been present they would at once have called their chicks away from such a dangerous acquaintance as a dog, and having been warned the little ones would afterwards have treated those animals with respect. That is an instance of the manner in which education often takes the place of instinct.

The promptness with which young birds obey their parents' warning cry in the presence of danger is very remarkable. If an old Pheasant be surprised while jauntily leading a string of fluffy chicks from a hedgerow into the open, it will itself, after uttering notes of warning, immediately disappear into the nearest cover. Not so the little ones; they instantly stand as motionless as if they were turned to stone, each one in the exact position in which it happened to be at the moment when the signal was given, and though you pass within a yard of them they will probably make not the slightest movement nor in any other way betray their presence. As soon as the danger has passed the old bird will rejoin her family and take charge of them again.

The instinct to remain motionless in order to avoid being seen is a very common one amongst chicks which are hatched on the ground and begin to run about almost immediately. Such chicks are clothed in down which usually matches the colour of their surroundings, and so may easily escape notice. This is called 'protective colouration.' Often there are stripes, patches, bands, or collars of a lighter or darker colour than the rest of the down, which aid the deception by making the owner look like two or more separate objects, such as stones or little lumps of earth, lying on the ground. Unlike the Pheasant chicks mentioned above, most of these birds drop flat on the earth and crouch there with their necks pressed close down. In that position they are practically unrecognisable unless you catch their

Stereo Copyright, Underwood & U. London and New York
BABY OSTRICH LEAVING THE EGG
The baby ostrich is one of the most precocious of chicks, and can run about as soon as it escapes from the egg, sometimes literally carrying a portion of the shell on its back. When it is born its feathers look very much like the spines of a hedgehog.

NURSERY DAYS AND EDUCATION

eye, and when they stand up again they seem to have appeared suddenly from nowhere.

Young Game-birds begin to practise standing on their feet very soon after they are hatched, and in a few hours can walk quite well. That is so even when they are hatched in an incubator, though in these circumstances they take about twice as long to learn as when they have a mother to look after them. Ducklings and Moorhens are more backward, and if they try to stand on one foot and scratch themselves with the other during the first day of their life they topple over, whereas an ordinary chicken can perform this feat of skill quite creditably.

Few young birds are more precocious than Ostrich chicks. These birds make their appearance from the eggs covered with a bristle-like growth which has very much the same appearance as the quills of a hedgehog, as you may see in the illustration opposite. They can not only run easily, but are quite capable of feeding themselves from the first, though it is said that they will not begin to pick up food unless they are taught to do so either by the old bird or by the person who has charge of them suggestively tapping on the ground in imitation of a bird pecking. It is certain that chicks of various kinds which have been hatched artificially can be induced in this way to begin feeding themselves, and the natives of Assam, who are in the habit of rearing newly hatched Pheasants which they find in the jungle, teach them to take their rice by tapping among it. It is said that without this help many would die.

But I think it is very likely that they would soon learn to help themselves, even if they were left to their own devices. At all events no such instruction was needed by a young chicken three days old, which until then had been kept carefully blindfolded. When the bandage was removed this little bird first of all sat and chirped for about five minutes, while it took a general view of the strange world in which it suddenly found itself. Very soon its attention was attracted by a fly some distance away; it then began pecking its own toes, and learnt to aim well so quickly

NURSERY DAYS AND EDUCATION

that a few moments later, on making a dart at the fly, which had crawled within reach, it seized and swallowed it at the first attempt. It next tackled and disabled a hive bee; but at the end of twenty minutes it had still not moved a step. On being placed within sight of a Hen and her brood, however, the little bird showed that it could use its feet as cleverly as its beak, for after chirping for a minute or so it made for the family party as straight as possible over the rough ground, leaping over small stones and running round larger obstacles without a single blunder.

Young birds are always more quickly attracted by moving food, and that is why a Hen picks up and drops in front of her chicks the grains of food which she wishes them to eat, even when they have learnt how to peck. Nestlings whose food is placed in their mouths by their parents cannot be taught to pick it up from the ground like chicks until they are much older; as a rule, all that they can do is to open their mouths very wide and wait for it to be given to them. Young Moorhens, however, which are fed from their mother's beak at first, will peck upwards at anything that is offered to them, but not downwards.

When a young bird has learnt how to take its food, it has to learn by experience what is nice and what is nasty, what is good for it and what is not. Here the mother's guidance is of great assistance, for the chick seems to have no instinctive knowledge of these things; it will peck at anything that is not too large, whether it be its own toes or a small stone, its companions' eyes or a maggot. Like a puppy which will attempt to swallow almost any object which is not disagreeable to the taste, even a piece of string, until it learns better, the young chick will try everything, test it in its bill, and store up its impressions for future use. In the case of two things which both have the same appearance, but one of which is pleasant to the palate and the other distasteful, such as yolk of egg and orange peel, the chick's behaviour depends on which of the two

NURSERY DAYS AND EDUCATION

is picked up first. If it be the nasty one, and it happens to have a very unpleasant flavour, probably nothing will induce the little fellow to taste the other which resembles it in appearance; but if he has the nice morsel first, he will afterwards probably try the nasty kind more than once before he gives it up in disgust; he is then, however, suspicious of the nice food too, and refuses it for some time, though he may eventually peck at it hesitatingly and give it another trial.

It is just the same in the case of insect food; unless the mother is present to give warning, a chick has to learn by personal and perhaps painful experience what kinds may safely be eaten and what kinds have stings or are otherwise undesirable. But though young birds apparently have no instinctive knowledge of what is good to eat and what will lead to uncomfortable sensations, they are often preserved from painful consequences arising out of ignorance by a wholesome fear of anything big, especially if it buzzes. A bluebottle is as suspicious an object as a bee to a very young chick, who is often deceived by his noisy, blustering conduct into imagining that he is better left alone; but the deception does not last very long, and like other blustering fellows the fly is soon found out. A young Plover which will peck at a small worm is afraid of a big one. Old birds also are suspicious of anything of unusual size. If you have been in the habit of putting breadcrumbs on your window-sill for the Sparrows, try the effect some day of placing a large slice of bread there instead; it is quite likely that you will find the birds are shy and suspicious at first, and refuse to come near it until they have grown accustomed to such an unusual object and have made up their minds that it is not dangerous.

But although young birds are naturally cautious, they are of course further protected from the danger of taking improper food by their parents, who give them only what is good for them and often induce them to eat by making pretence of doing so themselves, just as a mother often persuades her child to eat

NURSERY DAYS AND EDUCATION

his dinner by pretending to take a spoonful to show how nice it is.

Unless young birds are taught to drink by their mother, they generally seem to learn quite by accident—that is to say, however thirsty they may be they do not recognise water by sight, but only find out by experience that *that* is what they want. The discovery may be made in various ways—by pecking at a dewdrop, or at some speck or grain in the water, or at the edge of the water where it is in tremulous movement, or at a bubble; the beak then becomes wet, and that seems to be enough to awaken the drinking instinct, for the little bird at once quenches its thirst after the manner of its kind. One chick will imitate another; but if there is neither an old bird to teach them nor a more forward youngster to imitate, they have to find out for themselves what drinking is, and they find out accidentally.

Young Ducklings appear to be no wiser. If they are not in charge of their mother, they will walk about for some time in shallow water without taking any notice of it until one of them finds out suddenly that it is good to drink. It is very interesting to learn that even the dogs which were born during the *Discovery* Expedition in the far south, and had never seen water except in the frozen state, did not know in the least what to do with it when it was first offered to them. They had always quenched their thirst by eating snow, and they grew very thirsty indeed before eventually they were taught to drink by having their noses forcibly thrust into the water.

Though young birds, newly fledged, cannot fly either as quickly or as confidently as their parents, and skill only comes with practice, they begin to use their wings instinctively as soon as the feathers are large enough to support them in the air; indeed, even before they are fledged they stretch out their little featherless wings if they feel themselves falling. Any one who cares to make a simple experiment with an ordinary chicken may see that this is so. The best way to do it is to

NURSERY DAYS AND EDUCATION

take a chicken not more than a day or two old and place it in a basket; then raise the basket as high as possible and suddenly lower it, and you will see the little bird at once open its wings, though they are not yet of the slightest use for preventing it from falling. A few days later the chicken not only spreads its wings, but flaps them as if in flight; and if frightened while on the ground, it flaps them as it runs in trying to escape.

The early flights of young birds seldom carry them very far, but some kinds are more successful than others in their attempts. Young Swallows are perhaps as clever as any; they launch themselves boldly from the nest, circling round and alighting again without a blunder. Others go through an elaborate course of training before they venture to attempt actual flight. Young Storks, for example, begin by moving round the edge of the nest flapping their wings; then they take a little jump and learn to support themselves for a moment in the air, rising higher at each attempt, but taking care always to keep over the nest until they are able to remain in the air for half a minute or more. Having at length gained confidence by this kind of practice, they glide out boldly from the margin and indulge in short flights around their home, and eventually they get sufficient courage to take refuge on a neighbouring roof.

Occasionally fledglings are too timid to attempt to fly until their parents urge them to make an effort. Usually a little gentle encouragement is all that is required, with the offer of something nice to eat as an inducement. I have often watched Sparrows fluttering before their young ones with a tempting morsel held in the beak, uttering persuasive calls; and Hawks frequently place the game which they bring home to their young just out of their reach when they are old enough to fly, and so tantalise them into taking their first lesson.

Persuasion, however, is not always effective in overcoming the young birds' timidity, and in that case their parents have to resort to sterner methods. Many a fledgling is compelled

NURSERY DAYS AND EDUCATION

to take its first flight by being turned out of the nest, neck and crop. House-Martins are said sometimes to drag out their laggard children with their beak; and such birds as Falcons and Eagles vigorously insist on their family leaving home as soon as they are old enough to look after themselves.

Water-birds, also, exercise a wholesome discipline over their young, in compelling them to practise swimming and diving. The young birds, however, are usually very precocious, and they never have to learn *how* to swim. Many of them are extraordinarily skilful in the art almost from the moment when they leave the egg. Young Moorhens swim before they can walk, and though their first strokes are rather sprawly, they soon get the correct Moorhen action. In South America there is found a bird called the Jacana (*Parra jacana*), whose habits are very similar to those of our Moorhen, but whose swimming powers at birth are even more remarkable, as Mr. Hudson accidentally discovered. On a certain occasion, while examining a Jacana's egg which he had just removed from the nest, he found that the shell was already chipped and the chick about to make its escape. The old birds were greatly excited, and poured out their loud cries with a sound very much like a policeman's rattle; perhaps their calling stirred up the chick to make a great effort, for the shell suddenly parted and the young bird leaped into the water. Although that was its first moment of life outside the egg, it immediately behaved like a practised swimmer, stretching out its neck and paddling quickly to a neighbouring mound, where it hid itself in the grass, lying perfectly still like a young Plover.

A curious fact of which few people are aware is that ordinary domestic chickens a day old can swim quite well until their down becomes sodden, but as they grow up they lose this instinctive skill, and an adult Hen floats about and struggles aimlessly if she finds herself in deep water. It is a remarkable circumstance, too, that if young water-birds, such as Ducklings, are kept away from the water beyond the usual time for begin-

NURSERY DAYS AND EDUCATION

ning to swim they rather shrink from it at first; the moment they get a ducking, however, the hereditary instinct is aroused and they know exactly how to behave—at all events when the first feeling of surprise has passed away. Those that are hatched in nests surrounded by, or close beside, the water usually take to an aquatic life almost immediately, while others are led down to the water by their parents as soon as they are old enough to undertake the journey. It is only the latter that require persuasion or compulsion before they will make the plunge. Young Penguins are not conducted to the sea until they have doffed their baby plumage, but when that time comes they are pushed rudely in by the old birds in spite of their protests. Eider-Ducks are introduced to their new element in a gentler and more scientific fashion, the mother taking them on her back and swimming a few yards with them, whereupon she dives and so fairly launches them, to sink or swim by their own efforts. Dabchicks take their little ones under their wings and hold them there while they dive. The chicks are excellent swimmers, but are disposed to board their parent on every opportunity; if they become too troublesome they are chastised with a sharp peck.

A Dabchick's nest is a sodden mass of weeds, so the very young chicks are brooded and kept warm on their mother's back, under the wing, until they are old enough to sleep on the water like their parents. This is of course the exact opposite of the ordinary way, the vast majority of nestlings being kept warm and dry in the nest by the old bird brooding *over* them. Nearly all very young birds, especially those that are born naked, have to be protected from rain lest they should die of cold. When a heavy shower comes on while the mother is away collecting food, she hurries home and sits upon the nest with half-spread wings, thus forming a shelter from which the raindrops trickle away.

Young chickens begin to pay attention to their toilet almost as soon as they can stand, and I have many times watched

NURSERY DAYS AND EDUCATION

them in an incubator a few hours after being hatched arranging and combing the down on their breast and shoulders. Bathing, too, whether in water or dust, is instinctive.

It seems probable that young song-birds remember something of their parents' song from hearing it during their early days in the nest. We know that song is not altogether instinctive, as call-notes are, but is to some extent learnt by imitation, because a young bird which is hatched in captivity by birds of another species learns the song of its foster-parents; thus a Skylark hatched by Linnets learns the Linnet song. But if the little bird spends the first few days of its life in the nest of its real parents it never quite forgets the notes of its own kind.

There is reason to believe, too, that young birds keep a dim remembrance of the architecture of the nest in which they were hatched, and that this early memory helps them, when instinct leads them later on to set up house on their own account, to build nests like those of the rest of their kind. But some nests are very complicated, and it is impossible to tell how they are constructed merely by looking at the outside, so there is little doubt that imitation of other birds plays its part here also, and both early memories and imitation are probably assisted by an instinctive tendency to build in a certain fashion. Young Moorhens are remarkable, as we shall see later, for practising nest building while they are still chicks.

Nests are of almost infinite variety and of all degrees of elaborateness or simplicity; indeed, the only character which they invariably possess is more or less roundness in shape. As many different kinds were described in *The Romance of Animal Arts and Crafts*, and there are so many other interesting things to be told about birds and their ways, we will not say more here on a subject which might easily fill the whole volume. Many birds build no nest at all, but lay their eggs in holes or on the bare ground. Eggs which are laid in holes are

NURSERY DAYS AND EDUCATION

usually white, or have very few markings, because being hidden from sight it does not matter how conspicuous they are, while eggs laid on the ground without any concealment are covered with spots or patches or stripes which render them very difficult to see from a little distance; the latter, in short, are protectively coloured, like the precocious chicks which we mentioned earlier in this chapter.

The birds which are most extraordinary in their nesting habits are undoubtedly the Cuckoo and a few others of similar proclivities. The Cuckoo, as is well known, places each of its eggs in the nest of some bird of another species—the Pied Wagtail, for example, or the Titlark or Hedge-Sparrow—and leaves it to the care of the rightful owner of the nest. The egg is first deposited on the ground, from which the Cuckoo afterwards takes it up in her bill and, seizing an opportunity when the Wagtail or other bird is not at home, cautiously places it amongst the eggs already contained in the nest. In course of time the young Cuckoo is hatched, and then a dreadful tragedy is enacted, for this bird enters upon a career of misdoing in its earliest infancy. It is an ugly youngster, without a vestige of a feather, its eyes are not yet opened, and its thin neck is apparently too weak to support its unprepossessing head; but in spite of its blind and naked condition it is able by a wonderful instinct, aided in all probability by an extraordinarily developed sense of touch, to carry out the murderous eviction of all its foster brothers and sisters or of any eggs that remain unhatched.

The earliest account which we have of the exact way in which the deed is performed is that of the great Jenner, known to fame as the discoverer of vaccination, whose observations have many times been corroborated in the most minute detail. The young Cuckoo struggles about in the nest until it gets its broad, shovel-shaped back under an egg or one of its fellow tenants; it then climbs backwards up the side of the nest and, standing with its legs straddled well apart,

NURSERY DAYS AND EDUCATION

heaves its burden on to the edge, completing the business by elbowing it fairly over the margin with its featherless wings. Having made sure by feeling about that it has really gone overboard, the blind little monster sinks to the bottom of the nest and rests until sufficiently recovered to hoist another victim on its shoulders and thrust it out in the same manner. In this merciless fashion all are sacrificed, and the usurper remains in sole possession of the nursery.

Not the least strange part of the story is that the birds whose young he has murdered make a spoilt child of him. He becomes the sole object of their solicitous care and thrives under their devotion. Even when fully fledged and considerably larger than his hard-worked foster-parents, the overgrown youngster continues for some time to receive stolidly every insect that they can bring him. To see him receiving their dainty offerings is a ludicrous spectacle, for often they have difficulty in reaching his bill, and are obliged to perch between his shoulders in order to put the food into his cavernous, orange-yellow mouth.

From the examples we have given it will be clear that a newly hatched nestling is possessed of a wonderfully complex automatic machinery which enables it, when exposed to certain conditions, to perform instinctive acts with a great amount of skill. But we have also seen that young birds learn by experience and imitation, and that they are even taught many things by their parents. In this way instinct becomes to a great extent replaced by intelligence; and the more intelligent the bird, the longer the education through which it passes in its early days before it is able to look after itself and make its own way in the world.

CHAPTER II

SITTING

Incubation period—Division of labour—Domesticated husbands—Swifts—A rebellious hen—The cloistered Hornbill—Manner of leaving and returning to the nest—Protective colouration—Scene in a heronry—Pelican Island—Incubation under difficulties—Cold and heat.

AFTER an egg has been laid, as everybody knows, it must be kept warm for a certain length of time, amounting in most cases to two or three weeks, before the chick is hatched. No less familiar is the method by which this is effected, and there are few phases of bird-life which are easier to observe. Anybody may, if they care to do so, see a Hen upon the nest, brooding over her eggs with feathers puffed out and wings slightly drooped, covering them patiently hour after hour with her warm body, leaving them only for a brief interval from time to time in order to feed, and, after making a hurried meal, returning anxiously to her treasures to renew her long vigil, until at last, on some wonderful day, her patience is rewarded and she emerges from her obscurity in all the pride of motherhood, surrounded by a brood of tiny chicks. We all know this, so why have a chapter about brooding? Is there anything more to be said on such a very commonplace subject? Yes, there is a great deal to be told—far more than we have space for here—and I think we shall find that, like most pages from the life-history of a bird, the more we know of it, the more interesting it becomes.

The period of incubation, as it is called—the period that elapses between the moment when the bird begins to 'sit' and the hatching of the egg—varies greatly with different kinds of

SITTING

birds. The domestic Fowl usually takes just three weeks, but its near relative, the Pheasant, takes several days longer. Most of our little songsters hatch their young in about a fortnight, and some small birds only require ten days; but a Swan must brood upon her eggs five weary weeks or longer, and the great Condor has to wait almost two months before her hungry offspring emerges from the shell. It is usually supposed that weather and climate have something to do with the length of time required for the hatching of the eggs—that the same sort of eggs will hatch sooner in warm weather than in cold, in a hot climate than in a cool one; but about this we really know very little, though it seems probable that these things may make some little difference.

We are accustomed to speak of the brooding bird as "she," and we are seldom wrong in doing so, for in almost all cases the female takes the principal if not the only part in the duties of incubation. If we turn to the most primitive and least intelligent of the birds, however, we find just the opposite state of affairs; with them it is the male who takes upon himself these duties, while his spouse enjoys a life of freedom. A little higher in the scale, amongst birds of rather more intelligence, cock and hen share the brooding between them, but we already find the female performing the greater part of the work and her partner acting only as assistant. When we come to the most highly developed and most intelligent of birds, the wife undertakes the brooding, while the husband feeds and tends her and occasionally relieves her for a little while; he watches over her, warns her of danger, protects her, entertains her, sings to her, and generally behaves to her like a good husband. A charming and, so far as we are aware, quite unique characteristic of the domestic life of the Hawk-Owl (*Surnia ulula*) has been noticed by Mr. Seebohm, who states that sometimes both the parent birds are found sitting upon the nest in company.

It is interesting to find that in all cases in which the hen is larger and more brightly coloured than her mate, she consist-

SITTING

ently shirks her duties, and he takes her place in sitting upon the eggs. There are not many such birds, and of these but a single species nests in Great Britain—the Red-necked Phalarope (*Phalaropus hyperboreus*). The Phalaropes are amongst the most graceful of birds, and are allied to the Plovers, but, unlike those birds, they are equally at home on land or water. Their nest is placed on the ground, among heather or herbage, and when the male bird is brooding over the four pale-brown, dark-spotted eggs, he is so faithful to his charge that he will hardly leave them to escape being trodden upon. Indeed, these birds are extraordinarily tame; and it is unfortunate for them that they are so, for they fall easy victims to the collector, and the race is rapidly becoming extinct in Britain. That is a fate which has already overtaken their relatives the Dotterel and the Godwit, which now only come to us as occasional visitors. Both these birds resemble the Phalaropes in the male being smaller than the female and performing the office of brooding, in which his partner takes no share. In the seventeenth and eighteenth centuries the Godwit was a famous table delicacy and was netted in great numbers; at the same time it was being robbed of its resorts in the fens by drainage, so that it is now lost to us. The Dotterel, one of the most beautiful of the Plover kind, has shared the same fate; and we have thus, through their trustfulness and our own folly, deprived ourselves of three of the most charming of birds. The word Dotterel means 'Little Dolt'; whether the bird owes its name to the ease with which it is caught, or to the eccentric behaviour of the male in sitting on the eggs while his wife wanders abroad, or to both, we cannot say.

Some birds, amongst which are the Owls, occasionally begin to brood as soon as the first egg is laid. Owls are not quite so wise as they look, but in their domestic arrangements they would certainly appear to display much wisdom if there were any reason to suppose that they could foresee the result of their action. It is clear that the eggs which are first laid and

SITTING

brooded over will hatch before those which are laid several days later, and this is an advantage to the parents in two ways. In the first place, it makes it easier for the old birds to provide for their young; and, further, the warmth of the earlier chicks helps to incubate the eggs which are still unhatched while the father and mother are both away hunting for food. But the plan would not do at all in the case of birds which can run about almost as soon as they are hatched, because the parent bird would not be able to brood over the eggs and to take charge of her precocious children, both at the same time. We find, therefore, that birds such as Pheasants and Plovers never begin to sit until all the eggs have been laid.

We have already mentioned that the cock often keeps the hen company and sings to her when she is on the nest. He may sit on a neighbouring twig while he pours forth his song; he may soar aloft like the Lark; or, like the Swift, he may call out a cheery greeting as he skims past her in rapid flight. This habit of the Swifts was, I believe, first noticed by Gilbert White. The Swift is especially lively in sultry, thundery weather. "In hot mornings several, getting together in little parties, dash round the steeples and churches, squeaking as they go in a very clamorous manner; these, by nice observers, are supposed to be males, serenading their sitting hens; and not without reason, since they seldom squeal till they come close to the walls or eaves, and since those within utter at the same time a little inward note of complacency."

In the evening, however, after the hen has been sitting all the day in her dark nest, she darts out in the fading twilight and "stretches and relieves her weary limbs, and snatches a scanty meal for a few minutes, and then returns to her duty of incubation." But she does not always return very willingly; sometimes the joy of that mad flight is too fascinating for her, and she cannot make up her mind to return to the narrow hole under the eaves. And so her flight is prolonged, until her husband has to interfere. He dashes after her to remind her

SITTING

that she really must be going home—that she has already been out too long, and that the eggs are growing cold; and will she please come back this very minute?

Mr. Hudson[1] describes how he watched the Swifts at Seaford going through this interesting performance. He says: "It was curious and amusing to see a pair in some cases, the hen-bird wildly rushing away, the mate in mad pursuit, and then when with infinite pains she had been driven home suddenly dashing off again, and the wild chase about the sky beginning afresh. Once I saw the hen-bird break away four times after being brought to the breeding-hole; but after the fourth time she remained in the nest, and the good, zealous husband went away to enjoy himself. A swift chasing his wife home in the evening can easily be distinguished from one swift chasing another swift for fun, or whatever the motive is that keeps them in a perpetual hunt after one another. He follows her closely in all her mad flights and sudden doublings until he has got her face towards home, and then keeping close to her agitates his wings in a peculiar manner, at intervals gliding smoothly, uttering all the time a measured sharp clicking chirp—a sound as of repeated strokes on a piece of metal."

The Hornbills (*Bucerotidæ*), birds with an immensely developed bill surmounted by a curious outgrowth called the *casque*, are given no opportunity of playing truant when they should be keeping their eggs warm, for the hen-bird is carefully imprisoned by her mate in the hollow tree where the eggs are deposited, and must remain there until the young are almost fully fledged. The incarceration is effected by building up a strong barrier at the entrance, leaving only a narrow slit through which the hen-bird can protrude her bill to receive the food brought to her by her husband. This may appear a very tyrannous proceeding, but there is no reason to believe that the imprisonment is not quite voluntary, for the female often her-

[1] *Nature in Downland*, p. 201.

SITTING

self assists in building the wall, which serves to protect her against the attacks of monkeys and large lizards. The male bird is very attentive, and the way in which he feeds his wife is one of the most remarkable features in the life of these strange birds.

Their diet is strictly vegetarian, consisting of various kinds of grape- and berry-like fruits. These are collected by the husband and brought home to his wife, and so far there is nothing extraordinary in the proceeding, for many birds practise this courtesy. What is so remarkable in the case of the Hornbill is that the fruit is offered in a neat little purse-like bag! The bag is about the size of a fig, which it resembles also in shape, and is made of some elastic material, so that it is neatly filled by the little collection of fruit which it contains. When first these curious bags of fruit were discovered they were a great puzzle to naturalists, but it was soon found that the bag is composed of the lining of the bird's gizzard, which becomes loosened and is cast off in one piece. We cannot wonder, therefore, that after feeding his partner for several weeks the devoted male is worn to a shadow by his self-sacrifice!

It is interesting to observe the various ways in which different species of birds leave and return to the nest. The departure is usually effected without ceremony, the bird flying directly from the side of the nest very quietly so as not to betray its whereabouts, but, as most boys are aware, some species, such as Blackbirds, are very clamorous and make a great fuss if they are surprised and frightened off the eggs while sitting. That, however, is not their usual method of leaving home; but there is clearly nothing to be gained by silence when the bird knows that its nest is already discovered. The Swallow-tailed Kite (*Elanoides furcatus*) has a peculiar way of rising straight up from the nest for a little distance, as if it were projected by a spring. No other bird behaves in quite the same manner, and its method of alighting is equally peculiar, for it hangs in the air a few feet above the nest with its outspread wings

SITTING

apparently motionless, and then lowers itself upon the eggs so gradually that it is difficult to say just when it alights.

Kites and other similar birds which build high in trees, or other inaccessible places, and are strong enough to defend their homes against winged marauders, need not attempt to conceal their goings and comings, but it is different with the ground-builders, whose safety depends entirely on their success in escaping observation. Many of these birds make hardly any nest—some, indeed, have none at all—and the colour of their eggs is in such perfect harmony with that of their surroundings that it is very difficult to detect them unless you know the exact spot in which to look for them. Frequently the birds themselves are also protectively coloured, so that it is only when they are moving that they are at all likely to be discovered. Such birds as these have quite a different method of going and coming. In the first place, they seldom fly directly from the nest, but run a little distance before rising from the ground. I believe the Skylark, to take a familiar example, always does this, and I have never seen one alight directly upon its nest.

Some of the larger ground-nesting birds are extremely cautious in their movements, but their methods differ even in the same species. A remarkable instance of this is afforded by the Stone-Curlew (*Œdicnemus scolopax*), one of our summer visitors which is met with chiefly in Norfolk and on that account is often spoken of as the Norfolk Plover. It is one of the largest of the Plovers, and resorts to barren, stony ground with scanty vegetation, where it lays its two eggs on a level spot, without the slightest attempt at a nest. The eggs so closely resemble in colour the sandy, flint-strewn surface that only a practised eye can detect them, and the drab, mottled plumage of the bird enables it to escape notice except at quite close quarters. Even then, as it squats with its neck outstretched close to the ground, it would usually pass unobserved if it would but keep its large, bright, golden eyes closed. Now

SITTING

this bird has two distinct methods of approaching its eggs. One way is to move very deliberately and stealthily, making long, slow strides, with its head held low. From time to time it pauses or remains perfectly still for several minutes, and proceeding thus it has frequently been seen by patient observers to take ten minutes or longer in arriving at the nest from a point only a few feet away.

The other method, which is only adopted, I believe, after the birds have begun to sit, is well described by Mr. Trevor-Battye in his *Pictures in Prose*. He says: "The pair of which I speak had chosen the middle of a gravelly space among the pines. By creeping up on hands and knees under cover of a bank one could gain a position, just fifteen paces away from the nest, without being observed: so close that with my glass I could see the light shine through the crystal prominence of the sitting bird's great yellow eyes. At intervals one bird would relieve the other on the nest. When disturbed the birds always ran for shelter to a bank beneath the pines. And here the bird that was not sitting always stood as sentry. When its turn came to relieve its mate it would walk pretty deliberately across the first part of the open, where it was more or less screened by a fringe of trees; and there, having reached a point that was commanded from a long way off, it would suddenly lower its head, and run as fast as a red-leg to the nest. When it was about a yard away the sitting bird would slip off and, staying for no greetings, run past and away to the pine-bank." Mr. Trevor-Battye noticed that the bird always rose from the nest *backwards*, and so avoided disturbing the eggs with its long legs. He also observed that "the new-comer did not turn the eggs immediately, but squatted perfectly still for perhaps a minute, as if to make sure it was not disturbed. And after the eggs were satisfactorily bestowed, and all the coast seemed clear, the bird would close its eyes in the hot sunshine and appear to go to sleep. But even then I could scarce move so much as a finger above the grasses, but instantly it was off its nest and away."

SITTING

This delightful picture of the domestic life of the Stone-Curlew introduces us to another interesting question of bird-life: the way in which a bird relieves its partner upon the nest.

Let us first take an instance of a home-coming from amongst the birds of our own land. When I was a boy I used occasionally to make a breathless excursion to a small heronry which was situated in the midst of carefully preserved lands in a midland county. Even now I have a vivid recollection of more than one such visit, for the way lay through hostile country where schoolboys did not meet with a very cordial reception, and the keeper, a thick-set man with keen grey eyes and a stone-wall expression—or perhaps *brick*-wall would give a more correct impression of his sunburnt complexion—was a danger to be reckoned with before venturing within the bounds; seen face to face at close quarters (it happened once), there was a positively painful suggestion of massive strength about him, and an even more discomforting suggestion in the short ash-plant (I never saw him carry a gun) which seemed to be a part of his awe-inspiring presence. I mention the keeper because he had a hut or shelter close by the heronry, and it was owing to this circumstance that I spent more time watching the birds than might otherwise have been the case.

Late one afternoon I had cautiously approached the heronry along a hedge and through a tangle of undergrowth when this much-dreaded person suddenly appeared outside his hut, and there was nothing for it but to lie hidden and await an opportunity to escape. Herons have learnt from sad experience to be the shyest of birds where man is concerned, but the members of this little colony must have decided that the keeper was their good friend. Now I think of it, I believe it was because, as I have already mentioned, he never carried a gun—nor did I ever hear a gun fired in the neighbourhood. At all events, the birds did not appear to be disturbed by his presence, and were certainly not nearly so much alarmed as the small boy crouching amongst the bushes.

SITTING

On that afternoon, watching alternately the leisurely movements of the keeper and the bird life around, I got to know more about the domestic life of Herons than I ever had an opportunity of learning for myself before or after, and amongst other things I was fortunate enough to see one of the birds return to the nest, where his partner had been patiently sitting, and take his place upon the eggs. All that had been visible of the sitting bird was her sharp bill, and occasionally her head and a portion of her long neck, outlined against the sky over the margin of the big nest of sticks near the summit of a tall elm tree, and it was a sharp movement of this tantalising object which first directed my attention to the returning bird. Looking towards the sky, I saw him sailing in the direction of the heronry in a grand downward sweep, his legs trailing out behind, his wings outspread and raised high above his back, and his neck bent in a sharp curve so that his head was drawn far back close to the body. As he drew near, his partner uttered a sudden harsh cry of greeting, which he answered by a wild scream as he stretched out his neck and came rushing down.

Just before he reached home his great hollow wings were brought smartly downwards to check his fall as he alighted and balanced himself on the edge of the nest; at the same moment, his mate stood up and they joined in a regular duet of screaming. Whether she was scolding him for being so late and he was explaining that it had taken him so long to get his dinner that he really couldn't help it, or whether they were just telling one another how glad they were to meet again, it was impossible to say. In any case, they soon became silent, and then the bird which had just arrived lowered his head and seemed to be carefully examining the eggs before bending his long legs and sinking down into the hollow of the nest. As he disappeared from sight his partner shook out her plumage and flew off, with slowly beating wings, towards the feeding-grounds, and again the voices of the small birds in the bushes below, unobserved while this interesting scene was being enacted, were

Stereo Copyright, Underwood & U.   *London and New York*

BROWN PELICANS AT HOME

Pelican Island, off the east coast of Florida, has been handed over to these birds by the American Government, by whom they are strictly protected. So many pelicans have set up house on the island that all the mangrove trees have been killed.

SITTING

the only sounds that broke the silence of the heronry. All this took place, as I have good cause to remember, late in the afternoon; the other change—for these birds only work two shifts during the whole of the day and night—occurs in the early morning soon after the sun is up.

On the east coast of Florida there is a muddy islet, not more than three or four acres in extent, which is known as Pelican Island because a colony of Brown Pelicans (*Pelecanus fuscus*) have annexed it for their very own. They are practically the only inhabitants, and their claim is backed up by the Government of the United States, who will not allow any one to interfere with the birds. Nobody is at all likely to want to take possession of their diminutive country, because it is little more than a mud-bank and only one little corner of that is really safe, for when the 'northers' come the waters sweep over the remainder of the islet and destroy scores of nests. The Pelicans, however, are a patriotic race and devoted to the land of their birth; no doubt they regard it as a very fine country indeed, for they return to it year after year for the purpose of bringing up their families. When they first landed the tiny islet was well grown with mangroves, which are equally fond of mud-banks; but so many Pelicans went to live there and built their nests upon them, that tree after tree was killed, and at the present time there is scarcely one remaining which does not present the desolate appearance which is shown so well in our photograph.

The birds arrive early in November, and within a month they have all set up house and are busy laying their two white, chalky-looking eggs. The husband and wife share the sitting between them, and when the time comes for changing over—which occurs at all hours of the day and with no sort of regularity—they go through quite an elaborate ceremony. Let us suppose that the male is coming home from his fishing. He alights near the nest where his partner is sitting, and with his great bill pointing straight up in the air he slowly advances,

SITTING

waving his head from side to side. His wife, on the contrary, sticks the point of her bill down into the nest, twitches her half-opened wings, and greets him with a husky, gasping "*chuck!*"—the only sound a grown-up Pelican can utter. Having saluted one another in this curious manner there is a pause in the proceedings, which is occupied by both birds preening and arranging their feathers. The male then steps on to the nest and settles down, while his spouse goes to bathe and attend to her toilet before setting out to catch fish for her dinner or to circle high into the air in one of the wonderful soaring flights for which these great birds are so famous.

A few birds, such as the Raven, display great hardihood in their endurance of cold when sitting. One of the most remarkable of these is the Great Horned Owl. In the northern States this is the first of all the birds to nest, and in spite of ice and snow it starts housekeeping about the end of January. On some tall forest tree, very often on the side of a hill, exposed to the full force of storms and blizzards, the hardy mother sits upon the rude platform of sticks which does duty for a nest, while the temperature is still far below zero. It sometimes happens that the eggs are frozen by the intense cold; in that case the bird merely buries them in the loose rubbish of the nest and, undiscouraged by the disaster, lays another set. The same nest may be used year after year, until at last it becomes so rotten that, incapable of supporting another family, it falls to pieces before the young are reared, and the little ones have to be brooded upon the bare bough.

Equally hardy, on occasion, is the Black Gyrfalcon (*Falco rusticolus obsoletus*). Mr. Turner, of the United States Signal Service, found that a pair of these birds had made their home at Fort Chimo on the ledge of a great rock which forms a precipice three hundred feet high. The nest was shut in by a regular palisade of ice columns, and could only be approached by a narrow space or doorway next the main rock; yet for nearly a fortnight the birds had been successfully incubating

SITTING

their four eggs in this ice chamber, better suited, one would have thought, for cold storage than for hatching!

Even this, however, is by no means the most extraordinary case of incubation under difficulties. In choice of time and place for nesting—if nesting it can be called—the eccentricity of the great Emperor Penguin of the Antarctic is unrivalled. Laying its single large egg amidst the darkness of a polar winter—when the thermometer sometimes shows a temperature of 100° Fahrenheit below freezing point, and the average for a month is but 50° higher than that—this strange bird spends the seven coldest weeks of the whole year in brooding over it; and the ground whereon it chooses to keep vigil in these cheerless circumstances is nothing in the world but sea-ice! To bring about a successful result and hatch a chick amidst such conditions very special and peculiar methods are necessary; but the difficulty, we need hardly say, has been solved in the evolution of these remarkable birds, otherwise they could never have acquired their extraordinary habit.

Given a bird, an egg, a field of ice, a temperature 50° below freezing point, and never a gleam of sunlight, the problem is to keep the egg warm enough for a chick to be produced from it. Could anything be more discouraging, or so apparently hopeless? You would suppose that the first essential would be that the bird should make a particularly warm nest in which to incubate. But without materials nest-building is obviously impossible, and as a matter of fact the Emperor Penguin dispenses altogether with such a luxury. The plan it adopts is to stand upright and keep the egg off the ice by placing it on the top of its large webbed feet, where it is held in position and covered by a heavily feathered fold of skin from the under side of the body, which hangs over it like a curtain and completely hides it. By this close contact with the body a sufficiently high temperature is maintained to bring about the development of a chick, which emerges at the end of the seventh week as queer-looking an object as one could well imagine, a pair of wide goggle-

SITTING

like rings round its eyes and a thick coat of down giving it a general appearance of being dressed for a motor journey.

Great heat is perhaps more often fatal to the nesting of birds than excessive cold. On the plains of India, if a Sand-Grouse be frightened from its eggs for any length of time they begin to cook under the fierce sun, and doubtless the same accident befalls other birds. But if Nature can devise means whereby an egg can be hatched in the terrible cold of an Antarctic winter, so too can she teach birds how to ward off the danger to incubation arising from tropical heat. Thus according to the Indians, Dr. Wallace tells us, the Gulls and Terns on the Amazon carry water in their beaks, during the heat of the day, to moisten their eggs (which are deposited in little hollows on the sand-banks) and keep them cool; and other birds are said to act on similar principles. This, however, introduces us to a subject which we must consider in the next chapter—the subject of incubation without body-heat.

CHAPTER III

BIRDS' INCUBATORS

Extremes of the brooding instinct—Aids to incubation—Sun-warmth: its advantages and dangers—Ostrich, Sand-Grouse, and Black-backed Courser—The Mound-Builders and their incubators—Maleos—Choice of ground—Hot springs—The buried chick—Brush-Turkey—Heat from fermenting vegetable matter—Attending to the incubator—Large feet of Mound-birds—Megapodes—Immense size of mounds—Ocellated Megapode—Precocity of Mound-bird chicks—Volcanic heat.

WE do not always sufficiently realise how very great is the variety of character exhibited by different kinds of birds and even by different individuals of the same species. I do not refer now to the more conspicuous aspects of their nature—the fierceness of the nobler Birds-of-Prey, the quarrelsome nature of that familiar rowdy, the Sparrow, the sociability of so many other Finches or of Parrots, and so forth —these are things which force themselves upon the attention of the least observant person. I am thinking rather of the domestic side of their lives, and more especially of their way of carrying out parental duties. As we have already been considering the question of incubation in the last chapter, it will be interesting and convenient now to give a few instances of the remarkable extremes of this instinct, and to show how some birds seem to be overcome by an irresistible longing to devote themselves to the tedious duty of brooding over a nest, while others manage to become parents without spending a single hour of their lives thus occupied.

In many birds the desire to 'sit' appears at some time or other to be quite overwhelming. I need hardly remind you of the obstinate way in which a broody Hen will insist upon settling down not only upon a nest of eggs, but upon anything which bears the slightest resemblance to an egg; she will be perfectly satisfied with a smooth stone in a quiet corner, if she can find nothing better. Once, in a disused barn, I came upon a Hen brooding over two potatoes, and from their appearance I have no doubt she had been sitting on them for several days— as happy, probably, as a child with a rag doll. And see how disconsolate our Hen is if we will not leave her in peace; how dejected she looks as she wanders about the farmyard, until at last she "goes off being broody," as the country people say.

A similar longing appears to take possession of the males of certain species during the breeding season. It is often seen in domestic Pigeons, and, as Mr. Dixon remarks, "the older a cock-pigeon grows, the more fatherly does he become. So great is his fondness for having a rising family, that an experienced unmated cock-bird, if he can but induce some flighty young hen to lay him a couple of eggs as a great favour, will almost entirely take the charge of hatching and rearing them by himself." Brehm, the famous German naturalist, somewhere describes the amusing situations which he observed in Lapland as a result of this instinct in the case of some Auks. Amongst these attractive birds the males are in the majority, consequently every year some of them are obliged, much against their will, to remain bachelors. About Easter-time the great flocks hurry back from the sea to reach the bergs where they were born—for these birds, like many others, seem always to return if possible to their birthplace, when they in their turn are intent on bringing up a family of their own. The more fortunate ones, that is to say those who have found mates, may be seen coquetting and indulging in playful caresses by the way, while the disconsolate bachelors keep them company.

On reaching the berg, they all, married and single, land, and the paired birds hasten to put their old nesting-holes in order or to make new ones. In due course a big, top-like egg appears in every burrow, and the happy parents take turns in brooding over it. What becomes of the bachelors meanwhile? They too would very much like to brood if they could but find a mate, but that is out of the question. So many of them attach themselves to some happy couple as friends of the family, and keep the husband company while he stands on guard before the nest on which his wife is brooding. From time to time, the husband takes a turn on the nest while his partner goes to the sea to fish, but his bachelor friend still mounts guard; indeed most of his leisure is spent in this way. It is when both partners visit the sea together, however, that he finds his opportunity and his reward, for on these occasions he eagerly enters the burrow and takes a turn at sitting upon the forsaken egg, only resigning the position when the owners return. As a result of this unselfish conduct orphans are unknown amongst these birds, just as they are unknown amongst the Penguins, for even if both parents come to grief, the bachelor birds are always ready to finish hatching the egg and to take charge of the chick during the weeks which pass before it is capable of attempting its first flight to the sea.

Now let us look at the other side of the picture. In striking contrast to the birds which we have been considering, there are others which so arrange matters as to get their eggs hatched without their own personal care and attention during the process of incubation—or, at all events, with as little as possible. The methods which they adopt to this end are of remarkable interest, and we may well devote the remainder of the present chapter to describing them. We are not concerned now with Cuckoos, which artfully foist their eggs upon other birds and leave them to their fate—we have already had something to say about *their* conduct; but with those birds whose eggs are incubated without the help of body-warmth, in much the same way as the eggs of domestic fowls are often nowadays hatched in an artificial incubator by the heat from a lamp, except that

BIRDS' INCUBATORS

the artificial incubators of the bird world are supplied with heat in a different way.

As might be supposed, it is only in very warm climates that birds' 'artificial incubation' could as a rule be carried on with any hope of success, and you will of course at once guess that one way in which it can be brought about is by the heat of the sun. Until recent years it was commonly believed that Ostrich eggs were always hatched in that way; but like many other popular ideas about the life of birds, this one is not quite true. The real facts are as follows.

The Ostrich, like its near relatives the Emus, Rheas, and Cassowaries—all, indeed, except the curious little New Zealand Kiwis, which nest in burrows—is content with very little in the way of a nest, which consists of nothing more than a slight hollow scratched in the ground. We know exactly how the Ostrich makes the nest hollow, and as it is as peculiar as everything else about this strange bird, it is worth describing.

You have no doubt noticed that when an ordinary domestic Hen wants to take a dust-bath in the warm weather, she often prepares for it by standing on the chosen spot and scratching up the dry earth with her claws until she has made a convenient little hollow in which she can crouch and flutter her feathers. Most birds which have occasion to scratch holes in the ground, whether for the purpose of dusting, searching for food, or providing a receptacle for their eggs, go to work in the same manner. Not so the Ostrich; he uses his immensely strong legs in quite a different way. Having decided where the nest is to be, with one of his wives (he usually has at least three or four) in attendance, he sinks down on his breast, and in that position proceeds to tear up the sand with powerful kicks, casting it behind him as he does so. When one part of the hole is deep enough, he turns round and continues the operation in another direction until he has made a circular hollow, about a yard wide. Meanwhile his wife stands by and looks on; now and then she makes some show of helping him by picking up a little sand in her beak and dropping it about the edges of the hole, but her part is mainly that of an interested spectator. The work is soon completed, and the result is a shallow pit, around which the loosened earth is heaped in a low bank. Against this bank, in due course, the outermost circle of eggs will rest. The hens now begin to lay, all in the same nest, each of them depositing an egg every other day, until there are from fifteen to thirty altogether. There may be as many more scattered around the nest, and these, as we shall see in another chapter, have their own peculiar use.

Until ten or a dozen eggs have been laid the nest is left unattended, both day and night, with no protection except a thin covering of sand against the deadly wild-beast foes which prowl about the desert tracts. When that stage is reached, however, the male bird begins to brood over the eggs, taking his place upon them at nightfall, surrounded by his wives. But the process of hatching is principally dependent upon the burning sunshine and the hot desert sand, for during the day the eggs are left in the pit unattended, covered as before by a thin layer of sand, while the birds go hunting for food or make long journeys in quest of water.

In the cooler portions of the country which the Ostriches inhabit, and on the South African farms, the heat of the sun is apparently not sufficient to enable them thus to play truant, for in these localities the hens brood by day. But from the boundaries of Barbary, throughout the tropical region towards the South, where the birds are in attendance, whether by day or by night, it would seem to be for the purpose of guarding their treasure from jackals and other small beasts of prey rather than from any real necessity for helping to keep the eggs warm.

Many birds besides Ostriches and their near relatives are relieved to some extent from the duties of incubation owing to the warmth of the sun in the countries which they inhabit: amongst them are the Sand-Grouse and other species that

BIRDS' INCUBATORS

make their home on deserts and sands. In some places, however, where the heat is very great indeed—in the hotter parts of India, for instance—we find the exact opposite to be the case; the birds are obliged to remain on the nest all day, exposed to the terrible heat, not because the eggs would grow cold if left to themselves, but because they would soon be cooked if they remained uncovered! According to Captain Verner, the Black-backed Courser (*Cursorius ægyptius*), which buries its eggs in the sand on the banks of the Nile, has found a more ingenious way out of the difficulty. The bird dips its breast in the river until the feathers are thoroughly soaked with water, and then presses it against the sand under which its eggs are concealed. In this manner the ground is kept moist, and the evaporation of the water prevents the sand, and therefore the eggs, from becoming overheated, just as those porous earthen jars which are used in Spain and other countries about the Mediterranean and elsewhere keep the water which is contained in them cool and fresh by evaporation of the moisture which percolates to the outer surface of the vessel.

All the birds which we have hitherto mentioned are mere amateurs in the making of artificial incubators compared with the order of which we have now to speak, that, namely, which consists of the various birds known as Mound-Builders.

Of these there are several kinds, and all of them are humble relatives of our Common Fowl, living in Australia and various islands from New Guinea to the Philippines. More than three hundred years ago travellers brought home wonderful stories of the strange habits of these birds, but naturalists were slow to believe them, regarding their accounts as mere 'travellers' tales' and nothing more. We know now that these old stories were fairly accurate as far as they went, and that they did not recount half the curious works which are wrought by the Mound-Builders.

The fact is, the birds of this strange order have discovered the art of making efficient artificial incubators which relieve

BIRDS' INCUBATORS

them entirely of the duty of brooding over their eggs. Some of them, it is true, merely bury their eggs in the ground, but even these are often remarkable for the skill with which they choose the sort of ground which will best suit their purpose; others, however, prepare elaborate structures which are begun many weeks before the eggs are laid.

An example of the first kind is the Maleo (*Megacephalon maleo*), first fully described by Dr. Wallace in his book about the Malay Archipelago. This bird inhabits the island of Celebes, and is the only Mound-Builder which is at all remarkable for its colour. Most of them are dull, plain-looking birds, but the Maleo has not only a glossy black and rosy-white body, but its bare neck is bright red, and on the back of its head it bears a peculiar ornamental knob, like a small helmet. The nesting-place described by Dr. Wallace was a large uninhabited bay between two islands, where a forest extends to the edge of a steep beach composed of loose black sand. All the rest of the beach is white, and the reason why this portion is black is that ages ago a great stream of lava from a neighbouring volcano here flowed down a valley to the sea, and it is by the breaking up of the lava that the black gravel has been formed.

To this unattractive spot numbers of Maleos repair year by year to deposit their eggs, in August or September, when there is seldom any rain. They fly down to the beach from the interior of the island in pairs, often travelling ten or fifteen miles; and when they arrive at the nesting-ground both birds begin to scratch a hole in the hot, black sand, just above high-water mark. The Maleo's toes are joined together by a strong web, forming a broad, powerful foot, and when the birds are engaged in digging the sand flies up in a perfect shower. In this way a hole three or four feet in depth is soon excavated, and at the bottom a single large egg is laid. After covering it over with about a foot of sand the birds return to the forest. In rather less than a fortnight they again go down to the beach in company and once more set to work at the same spot.

BIRDS' INCUBATORS

Another egg is then laid, very near to the first. The hole is partly filled in every time an egg is deposited, so the birds have to renew their labour at each visit. It often happens that many birds lay in the same hole, a dozen eggs, or even more, being frequently found together. The natives regard the eggs as a great delicacy, and visit the beach every year from a distance of fifty miles around on purpose to obtain them. They are richer than Hens' eggs, and as one of them is large enough to fill a fair-sized tea-cup it is sufficient, with a little rice or bread, for a very good meal.

Why, it may be asked, do the Maleo-birds choose the unattractive-looking black ashes in preference to the clean, white sand which covers the rest of the beach of Wallace Bay? The latter would seem to be far more suitable, for the ashes are rough and coarse, consisting of fragments of lava each of which is about the size of a bean. Perhaps there is some special advantage in the dark colour. Let us consider this. You know that if you wear a black jacket in very hot, sunny weather you feel much hotter than you do if you wear a white one; that is because black absorbs heat, while white reflects it; and here we seem to have the true reason why the birds choose the black gravel instead of the white sand, not only in Wallace Bay, but at other places on these shores where the same conditions exist. Everywhere, so far as we know, they show the same preference.

This is a wonderful instinct; but the Maleo-birds of the Bone Valley are even more sagacious. Here two cousins named Sarazin, both of them naturalists, came upon a great number of pits dug out quite close together in a bamboo thicket, and on a search being made several new-laid eggs were discovered. Now this valley is about seven hundred and fifty feet above the level of the sea, and the temperature is rather low, especially in the forest, so it seemed surprising that Maleo eggs left buried in the ground should ever produce chicks. Further on and at a still greater height—this time about one thousand five hundred

BIRDS' INCUBATORS

feet above the sea—more diggings were found. What was the explanation? It was this: in the neighbourhood of the pits in each case there was a warm spring, the water of one of them being so hot that it caused the skin to smart and tingle when a hand was plunged in it, and these springs provided the necessary heat for the birds' incubators. Wherever Maleo-birds were found in the interior of the Celebes, warm springs were sure to be discovered not far away.

When the eggs have been buried the mother pays no further attention to them, but leaves them to hatch in the hot sand. Fortunately they require no attention, for even if they did it is difficult to see how the parents could remain to watch over them. Hundreds of birds visit this place to lay their eggs, and as their food consists entirely of fallen fruits, in search of which they are obliged to wander far afield, and the eggs are laid at such long intervals (about eight eggs are laid during the season, and it takes the bird three months altogether to produce them), the supply of food would be insufficient, and the birds would all very soon die of hunger if they remained in the neighbourhood of the beach. Besides this, owing to the continuous diggings the surface of the sand becomes not unlike that of a rough, confused sea, and is constantly changing in appearance, so that it is doubtful whether a bird would be able, after a short time, to discover the spot where she laid her first egg. And even supposing all the birds which bury their eggs in one hole were to stay beside it, they could not possibly know their own chicks when they made their way out of the ground.

One of the most remarkable circumstances about these birds, and others with similar habits, is that the chicks should ever escape from the mound at all. Any ordinary chick—a young Turkey, for example—would be quite helpless if it found itself buried alive when it escaped from the shell; but not so the young Maleo. We have already mentioned that the eggs are very large, and we find that the chicks produced from them are fine, vigorous youngsters from the moment they are born.

BIRDS' INCUBATORS

Somehow or other they work their way up through the sand and run off at once to the shelter of the forest. The young Mound-Builder, whatever the species, is one of the most precocious of bird children.

The actual manner in which the chick makes its way to the surface has been observed in the case of the Brush-Turkey (*Talegallus lathami*), another of the Mound-birds. Mr. Barnard, of Coomooboolaroo, a Queensland squatter and the head of a family of naturalists, buried an egg and allowed it to incubate in a heap of manure. A few days later he went to inspect it, and on carefully removing the covering he found a little bird within a few inches of the surface, lying on its back and trying to work its way out by means of its feet. His sons also on several occasions discovered young Brush-Turkeys in the same posture, when they were digging for eggs. This species is one of the largest of the Mound-Builders, being nearly the size of an ordinary Turkey-hen. Its plumage is sooty-brown in colour, but the skin of the neck is pinkish-red and the bird possesses a large, bright yellow wattle just above the breast. The incubators made by the Brush-Turkeys are on quite a different principle from those of the Maleos.

Instead of merely digging holes and burying their eggs where they will be hatched by the heat of the sun, the Brush-Turkeys construct huge mounds of leaves and grass mixed with earth, and the warmth produced by the vegetable matter as it ferments and decays enables the eggs to develop. If you will make a hole in a heap of grass which has been piled up in warm weather while still wet—cuttings from a lawn-mower, for instance—and left to rot, you will be able to observe for yourself how much heat is produced by the process of decay. This species of Brush-Turkey spends several weeks in collecting the material for its mound, and by the time the eggs are laid it has built a pyramid which is often large enough to make many cartloads. Of course one bird cannot do all this; at least a pair of them join forces to make one of the smaller heaps, and the

BIRDS' INCUBATORS

larger mounds may be the result of the united labours of several pairs. Besides this, the birds return to the same spot season after season, and add fresh material every year, so the heap goes on increasing in size.

Gould, that famous old writer about Australian birds, says: "The materials composing these mounds are accumulated by the bird grasping a quantity in its foot and throwing it backwards to one common centre, the surface of the ground for a considerable distance being so completely scratched over that scarcely a leaf or a blade of grass is left. The mound being completed, and time allowed for a sufficient amount of heat to be engendered, the eggs are deposited in a circle at the distance of nine or twelve inches from each other, and buried more than an arm's depth, with the large end upwards; they are covered up as they are laid, and allowed to remain until hatched. I have been credibly informed, both by natives and settlers living near their haunts, that it is not an unusual event to obtain half a bushel of eggs at one time from a single mound. . . . Some of the natives state that the females are constantly in the neighbourhood of the mound about the time the young are likely to be hatched, and frequently uncover and cover them up again, apparently for the purpose of assisting those that may have appeared; while others have informed me that the eggs are merely deposited, and the young allowed to force their way unassisted.

"One point has been clearly ascertained, namely, that the young from the hour they are hatched are clothed with feathers, and have their wings sufficiently developed to enable them to fly on to the branches of trees, should they need to do so to escape from danger; they are equally nimble on their legs; in fact, as a moth emerges from its chrysalis, dries its wings, and flies away, so the youthful *Talegallus*, when it leaves the egg, is sufficiently perfect to be able to act independently and procure its own food."

These birds have on several occasions made their mounds at

the 'Zoo,' and the eggs have been successfully hatched. It was there noticed that an opening was always preserved in the centre of the circle of eggs, probably to prevent the danger of a sudden increase of heat either from the action of the sun or from too rapid fermentation of the decaying vegetable matter in the mound. The male bird constantly attended to the incubator, and on hot days cooled the eggs by almost uncovering them two or three times between morning and evening.

The young birds remained in the mound for at least twelve hours without making any effort to escape, but on the second day they came out and ran about the pen for some time. They went to bed again early in the afternoon, however, and were carefully covered up for the night by their father. On the third day they could fly well. It does not of course follow that the birds behave in the same way in their natural condition as they do in captivity, where they are imprisoned in a pen and so compelled to remain constantly beside their mound.

At the 'Zoo' the male Brush-Turkey took a very active part in constructing the mound, and perhaps he always does so, though the evidence on this point is rather conflicting. If he does not, there is reason to suppose that he at least acts as foreman of the works. At the station of a squatter in Queensland there was a tame cock *Talegallus* which lived with the farmyard Hens. He was in the habit of driving his companions together into a little grove of trees near the house, and the owner of the station was convinced that he was trying to compel them to build a mound. The Hens, however, did not understand that kind of nest, and they seized every opportunity to escape from their taskmaster, but the *Talegallus* always chased them back again, until at last his insistence became so troublesome that he had to be shot.

A remarkable feature of the Mound-Builders is the great size and strength of their feet. This is not so noticeable in the Maleo as in other species; but then the Maleo does not make a true mound, but, as we have seen, merely digs a hole in

BIRDS' INCUBATORS

which to bury each egg as it is laid. Yet even in this bird the claws, though short and straight, form a broad and powerful foot; they are strongly webbed at the base, and this feature, combined with the length of the leg. helps to produce an admirable instrument for scratching. The birds which make true mounds, however, must be capable of more than mere scratching; in order to pile up these great structures they need a foot which can actually take hold of the material and fling it to a distance. So we find that the Brush-Turkeys have claws which are long and curved. The foot reaches its greatest development, however, in the Megapodes—a name which would at once lead you to expect a foot of more than common size.

All the Mound-Builders belong to the family of Megapodes, but the true Megapodes—the *Megapodii*—form a little group, a *genus*, apart from the Brush-Turkeys (*Talegalli*) and the Maleo-bird (*Megacephalon*). They have the most strongly developed 'scratching' organs to be met with in the whole of the bird world, and they know how to make good use of them. The birds themselves are about the size of small Hens, with very short tails, and though many of them have a crested head, their plumage is on the whole of a very dull and sober hue. Some of them construct immense mounds; the Australian Megapode (*Megapodius tumulus*), for instance, piles up material until it produces a hillock which not uncommonly measures as much as sixty feet in circumference, and sometimes a great deal more—a tremendous achievement for a bird. It is not to be supposed that one bird, or pair of birds, accomplishes such a gigantic labour in a single season; as in the case of the Brush-Turkeys, the Megapodes repair year by year to the same spot to deposit their eggs, and several pairs contribute to the building of the larger mounds; but even allowing for these circumstances, we must still be astonished at their extraordinary dimensions. Perhaps we shall get a better idea of their size from a remark of Macgillivray's: he tells us that some very ancient mounds have trees growing upon them, and he observed that in one instance the tree had a trunk which was a foot in diameter! All this sounds like a story from Gulliver's travels in the country of the Brobdingnagians—all except the very modest size of the bird itself, which only makes the story more wonderful still.

This Megapode is not at all particular about the nature of its building material, which varies according to the situation. The mounds are almost always near the edge of water. Many of them are found on the seashore and are composed of sand and shell heaped together in irregular masses, so that anybody who was not acquainted with their nature might suppose that they had been piled up by a heavy sea.

In such mounds there is nothing to develop heat, and the hatching of the eggs depends entirely on the warmth which they obtain from the sun. Others are found in neighbouring thickets or about the banks of creeks, and contain, as we might expect in these situations, fragments of decaying wood mixed with vegetable mould, the whole forming a cone-shaped mass which rather reminds one of a tiny volcano, especially when a crater-like hole has been dug in the summit by the birds when they come to deposit their eggs—or by the natives who visit the spot to rob them. There is a picture of one of these 'nests' in *The Romance of Animal Arts and Crafts* which shows a native armed with a sharp stick in readiness to begin digging out a supply of eggs. In the Solomon Islands the eggs of Brenchley's Megapode (*M. brenchleyi*) are very highly appreciated as an article of food. Mr. C. M. Woodford saw hundreds of these birds scratching out their holes in the warm sand when he landed at Savo, and they were so tame that they took very little notice of him. In this island, indeed, they become almost domesticated, and quietly go about their business of digging within a few yards of the native who is similarly engaged with the intention of getting possession of their eggs. They are so numerous here that thousands of birds congregate at the same

BIRDS' INCUBATORS

place and form great laying-yards which often extend over several acres. These are open, sandy spaces on which no shrubs or undergrowth can obtain a hold, chiefly because the ground is continually being dug over by the birds. I think we must regard these clearings as the largest of all the bird 'incubators.'

The most scientifically constructed incubator, however, is that made by the Ocellated Megapode (*Lipoa ocellata*) of Australia, but as there is a full account of it in another volume of this series, and also a picture, we will here describe it quite briefly. The way this bird makes its incubator is by first scratching a hollow in the ground and then building in it a cup-like mass of leaves, dead grass, and similar material. The whole is buried under a heap of sand, and the decaying vegetable matter soon begins to warm up the incubator. Seven or eight eggs are then laid in the sand in a circle, just inside the rim of the cup—which we may, perhaps, call the heating apparatus of the incubator—a hole being dug by the birds for this purpose on each occasion when an egg is deposited, and then carefully filled up again with sand. It is curious to note that here again the eggs are not placed on their side like those of other birds, but in an upright position with the smaller end downwards. It would be interesting to know why this is so. We know that such eggs as those of a Plover are always placed in the nest with the pointed end turned towards the centre because in that position they fit more closely together, and occupy less space than they would do if arranged in any other way, and are therefore more effectively covered by the sitting bird; but nobody, so far as I am aware, has been able to explain the peculiar position of the Mound-birds' eggs.

Mound-birds' eggs are often buried at a great depth. Those of the Australian Brush-Turkey are found more than an arm's length below the surface, and the Australian Megapodes' were taken by Gilbert from a depth of six feet in the mound. The Brush-Turkey, however, does not dig straight downwards, but

BIRDS' INCUBATORS

in a sloping direction towards the edge of the hillock, so that although the eggs are so far from the top, where the hole is always begun when the bird visits its incubator in order to lay, they might really be not more than two or three feet from the surface. But even if the young bird were to take the shortest way out of the mound, it would still have a great deal of burrowing to do, and it is surprising that it should ever be able to escape at all without assistance. Escape it does, however, though there is reason to believe that it sometimes remains buried a long time after leaving the egg. Some of the little birds which have been dug out are supposed to have been quite three weeks old when they were found; perhaps that is a mistaken estimate, but there seems no doubt whatever that many spend several days, at least, underground. One would expect them to die of starvation under such conditions, but on inquiry we find that occasionally, at all events, there is a supply of food conveniently at hand which may serve their needs during their imprisonment. When Gilbert first examined the mounds of the Ocellated Megapode he noticed that they contained large numbers of termites—the so-called 'white ants'—which had even made their little covered galleries upon the eggs themselves; so that here there was plenty of tender food ready for the chick as soon as it was hatched.

A young Megapode is not a naked, helpless being like many little birds when they are first hatched; it is not, like an ordinary domestic chick, merely clothed in down. It is a powerful youngster with strong limbs which are already capable of vigorous scratching; it has wings with fully developed feathers and can fly, if not as well as its parents, at all events well enough to enable it to escape easily in a very short time from its enemies. Why then does it choose to remain so long underground, in darkness, instead of making its way as quickly as possible to the surface? That is a question which has puzzled many naturalists, and one which we are still unable to answer.

BIRDS' INCUBATORS

Before leaving the fascinating subject of birds' incubators, as we have called them, we may perhaps mention a very curious instance, described by Dr. Merriam in his report on the Alaska Expedition, of the way in which the most tremendous forces of Nature may be of assistance in such a delicate process as the hatching of an egg. We have seen that the birds' incubators are kept warm in various ways. In some cases it is by the burning rays of the fierce tropical sun shining upon the dry desert sand, in some it is by the warming of the surrounding earth by hot-water springs, and in some by the heat produced when masses of dead vegetation, scraped together by the birds, ferment and decay. But there is yet another source of heat— a mighty source which, fortunately for us, only occasionally forces itself upon our notice, and which then is too often more apparently connected with destruction than with the fostering of life: the eternal furnace beneath the earth's crust. A little more than a century ago there appeared in the Behring Sea, amid thunder, earthquake and steam, a volcanic island now known as the Island of Bogoolof. This island had long been a favourite resort of countless multitudes of sea-birds when, in the year 1883, a companion volcano was thrown up from the sea.

The birds on the older island, the greater number of which were Murres, began to occupy the new land as soon as it was cool enough to afford a footing, and when Dr. Merriam first visited the island, eight years after its appearance above the waters, he found vast hordes in possession, standing by thousands on projecting points and ledges wherever the rocks were not too hot, and nesting there. No doubt the warmth of the rocks assisted the incubation of the eggs, but whether the birds took advantage of it to prolong their excursions on business and pleasure was unfortunately not ascertained. It seemed strange that the Murres should have chosen to make their homes in such a situation, for the sulphur fumes and hot steam were almost suffocating. The year after the volcano was

BIRDS' INCUBATORS

formed, many birds were observed to be killed instantly if they chanced to fly into the cloud of steam and smoke which hung over it, and even when Dr. Merriam called at the island he found lying on the rocks many dead birds which had evidently perished from the same cause—the victims, as in the case of so many human pioneers, of their own enterprise.

CHAPTER IV

FEEDING THE CHICKS

Infant-food and why it is necessary—Finches—Change of diet and special preparation of food—'Pigeon's milk'—Insect-eaters—Swallows and Swifts—A ball of flies—Reed-Warblers—Industry of parents—A working day of sixteen hours—Feeding the young in mid-air—Methods of giving food—An interesting experiment—Birds-of-Prey—Larders—Fish-eaters—Fish soup—Perverted instinct of domesticated birds.

WE are aware that some young birds, such as Partridge chicks, are able to pick up their own food very soon after they leave the egg; all that their parents have to do is to take them where food is to be found and, just at first, to place it in front of them and move it about in order to attract their attention: the rest they can do for themselves. Many little birds, however, are born quite helpless, and in the early days, or it may be weeks, of their existence are entirely dependent on their parents, without whom they would very soon die of hunger, just as surely as a young mammal would die if it were not suckled by its mother.

We are aware that the food on which mammals live when they are grown up would not be good for them when they are quite young; at that time they need something which does not require to be crushed and softened before it is swallowed and which is suited to the powers of little bodies not yet fully formed; and it is just the same with many young birds. We all know what a sharp, strong, and hard bill a Sparrow has when he is old enough to fly about and pick up a living in the street or farmyard, to eat the seeds we have just sown in our garden, or to rob the farmer of his corn. But the bill of a

FEEDING THE CHICKS

baby Sparrow which has just escaped from the egg is quite soft, and so is his stomach; his parents, therefore, acting instinctively as if they knew that seeds and berries and hard bread-crumbs would be injurious, give him nothing but soft food, and for a while he lives on worms and grubs and other delicacies. Sometimes the parents themselves take a fancy to a change of diet, and many hard-billed, seed-eating birds such as the Chaffinch become insect-eaters while they have a young family to provide for.

It is very interesting to watch the old birds when they visit the nest to feed their chicks, but it is often by no means an easy matter to do so. Frequently it is quite impossible, owing to the situation of the nest, to see at all what is going on there, and even in favourable circumstances it is often necessary to use a field-glass in order to get a good view. But if you are not discouraged by difficulties at first you will soon find that it is well worth while to take a little trouble.

On returning to the nest, some birds appear to have brought nothing at all back with them, but if we watch them closely we shall see that they presently begin to produce, one after another, caterpillars which are carried hidden away at the back of their throat. The Bullfinch, which is well known as a cage-bird—though less so now than formerly, I am inclined to think—and with which many of us are acquainted as an inhabitant of copses and bushy commons, has this habit.

Another way in which some of the seed-eating birds, such as the common Linnet, provide food adapted to the needs of their chicks, is by first softening the hard grain or seed in their own crops and thus producing what we may perhaps compare to a 'patent food for infants.' But a far more elaborate kind of infant-food is manufactured by those very dissimilar birds, Pigeons and Parrots. Different as they are in most respects, these birds resemble each other in so far as they are both strictly vegetarians, they both have particularly helpless babies, for whom they both produce this peculiar food.

FEEDING THE CHICKS

It is a whitish, half-solid, half-liquid material, rather like curdled milk in appearance, and on that account in the case of the Pigeon it has been called 'Pigeon's milk.' During incubation the lining of the bird's crop becomes thickened, and it is here that the 'milk' is produced in flaky curds. Just at first the young Pigeon is given no other kind of nourishment, but when it is a few days old a little partially digested food is mixed with the 'milk.' Then, as the young birds become bigger and stronger, the proportion of ordinary food is increased, so that by the time they are about a week or nine days old they are weaned from the 'milk' and are being fed entirely on ordinary food, which is still, however, softened for them by their parents. It is a curious fact that in the early days the old birds are able to force the 'milk' from the crop without any mixture of their own food, although later on both are mingled together.

The way in which a Pigeon gives food to its young is well known. It takes the bill of the squab (as a baby Pigeon is called) in its own and pumps up the soft food with a curious action familiar to all who have kept these birds as pets. The beak of a young Pigeon is well adapted for this kind of feeding, for it is not only soft and fleshy, but much thicker and larger in proportion to the size of the body than in after life. At first, indeed, it looks immense, but gradually, as the time approaches for the young bird to take to solid food and provide for itself, it shrinks and hardens.

It is interesting to note that both Parrots and Pigeons often show their affection for their mate by feeding her in the same manner. Parrots, indeed, as well as their near relations the Macaws and Cockatoos, sometimes go further, and produce food from their crop merely because they are very fond of the person who feeds them—an attention which is not always appreciated!

The Blue-bellied Parrakeet (*Psittacus cyanogaster*), as well as some others of the family, constantly feeds his mate while

FEEDING THE CHICKS

she is brooding, in the same way as the young. A pair of these birds observed by Levaillant continued for half a year to feed their two young ones, though the latter had left the nest when three weeks old—which, for Parrots, is very early. He states that it was a very interesting and beautiful sight to watch them, for the young would frequently be seated on a branch on the further side of their mother, and the male bird, being unable to reach quite so far, presented the food first to his partner, who immediately passed it on to the young.

Let us now take leave of the vegetarians amongst birds and turn to those whose ordinary diet consists of insects. Of these, the most familiar are probably Swallows and Swifts—not, we may remark in passing, coupled together here because they are closely related to one another, as they are so commonly and erroneously supposed to be, but merely on account of the similarity of their habits. Who has not watched these graceful birds on a summer evening skimming in long, beautiful curves through the air, sometimes high above our heads, sometimes, in the case of Swallows, quite close to the ground, in rapid, untiring flight? You may even have noticed the sharp little sound made by the snapping of their bills as, without the slightest interruption of their progress or slackening of speed, they capture a gnat or other minute insect—just what it is that they catch we can rarely tell, for though it is distinct enough to the birds' keen sight, to us it is invisible.

We will in imagination accompany one of these birds to the nest where a brood of hungry youngsters is awaiting its return. Suppose it is the Swift that we visit. That is much easier in imagination than in reality, for Swifts often make their nest in high towers, though occasionally they are less aspiring and are content to establish a home under a roof at no great height from the ground, as they did at my old school. The brood is a small one (two eggs being the usual number, though occasionally three are laid), but the old bird has been absent from the

FEEDING THE CHICKS

nest quite a long time, perhaps for a whole hour, so the chicks are very hungry; what has he brought them for supper? As he creeps in at the narrow opening under the eaves it is not apparent that he has brought anything at all, but there is a curious swelling under his chin which certainly looks as though he may perhaps have something hidden in his mouth. And so he has, for presently he opens his widely gaping bill and produces a round black object about the size of a boy's marble. What can it be?

I recollect, when I was a boy, catching a Swift which flew one evening through the open window of the schoolroom and was unable to find its way out again—the window having been promptly closed as soon as it appeared. And I remember how puzzled I was by the pouch-like swelling under its bill, until in its struggles the bird ejected from its mouth a huge pellet such as I have described, which, to my astonishment, I found to be composed of scores of small black flies all glued together in a solid mass. On the same occasion, before liberating the captive, I learnt for the first time that Swifts in their turn are persecuted by flies—horrible, wingless flies which infest their bodies, comfortably hidden away under the feathers, amongst which they glide with surprising rapidity if disturbed; and I still vividly recall my feeling of disgust on making this discovery and my pity for the victim of such loathsome parasites, which appeared of monstrous size to live on so small a bird. This, however, is a digression, and we must return to the subject of feeding the young.

Swifts, then, take to the nest a large number of flies at once, all stuck together in the form of a pellet or ball which is carried under the tongue. They therefore feed their chicks at comparatively long intervals, except just after they are hatched. Swallows and Martins, on the other hand, are continually feeding their families (which are more numerous than those of the Swifts) and may be seen returning to the nest every two or three minutes. In this they resemble the greater number of

FEEDING THE CHICKS

insectivorous birds, whose industry in supplying the needs of their young is almost incredible.

On the opposite page you will see a charming illustration of a pair of Reed-Warblers clinging to the reeds over their nest and looking down upon their family which they have just been feeding. It is from a photograph of the living birds, taken in a reed-bed beside an old fish-pond a few miles from Cambridge. Photographing birds in their own haunts is work which requires much time, and patience too, but it has the advantage of affording ample opportunities of observing their habits. Mr. Farren, who took this particular photograph, was watching the Reed-Warblers for an hour and three-quarters, and during that period they visited the nest at least thirty-six times, bringing with them caddis-flies, little Cambridge-blue dragon-flies, and other insects. That works out at about twenty visits in an hour; and on almost every occasion the birds brought food with them. The feeding is continued throughout the day, from sunrise to dusk—a summer-day-long feast of hundreds of courses! Imagine the energy and industry of the little birds which provide such a meal.

We do not merely *suppose* that the birds never rest from their labour of love all through the day, for patient naturalists have often kept a nest under observation from early morning until the time of roosting, and have made a note of every occasion when the parents brought food. In this way Professor Weed of Durham, New Hampshire, found that a pair of Chipping-Sparrows—American birds much like our Sparrows in general appearance, but considerably smaller, and familiarly known as 'Chippys'—between five minutes to four in the morning and half-past seven at night made almost two hundred visits to the nest, and during this busy day they brought food —soft-bodied caterpillars, crickets, crane-flies, and other insects —on nearly every occasion, though sometimes they returned with what appeared to be grit for the grinding of the food. There were no long intervals when the birds were not at work;

DEVOTED PARENTS: REED-WARBLERS AT HOME

Reed-Warblers build their nest over the water, weaving the walls securely round the supporting reed-stems   When the young are hatched the birds spend the whole of the long summer day in feeding them. returning every two or three minutes with their bills full of insects.

FEEDING THE CHICKS

the longest was twenty-seven minutes, and in the middle of the day as many as twenty-one visits were made in the hour.

But to return a moment to our Reed-Warblers. Mr. Farren writes: "It was very interesting to watch the olive-plumaged little birds working among the reed-stems; flitting from reed to reed, they would disappear through the jungle behind the nest, returning in two or three minutes with their bills full of insects and, clinging sideways on the upright reeds above the nest, reach down and deliver to the young the food they had brought. While attending to the nest each parent had its favourite perch; the female, which was the more industrious of the two, always settled on the reeds on the left of the nest, while the male kept to the right. The male also perched lower down than did the female; in fact, at times the latter bird clung to the reed so high above the nest that she could only reach the open mouths of the young ones by hanging in a position which may very well be described as 'upside down.'" She could apparently swing herself into almost any attitude without changing the position of her feet.

The moment when a bird has just given food to the young is with nearly all small kinds the surest time to get a good photograph, because it then usually remains for a second or two quite still, watching the chicks.

With regard to the Swallow, there is a remarkable circumstance in connection with the manner in which it gives food to its young which we have so far omitted to mention. When the fledglings are old enough to leave the nest they are fed for a day or so on the chimney-top, after which they are taken a little further afield, often to a dead branch of a tree, where they sit in a row and are waited on by their parents. Their education is progressing, but they are still unable to capture their own food, although by this time they will have learnt to fly, and it is at this stage in their upbringing that we may see the pretty act so well described by Gilbert White—the young being fed by their parents while on the wing. "They play

FEEDING THE CHICKS

about near the place where the dams are hawking for flies; and when a mouthful is collected, at a certain signal given, the dam and the nestling advance, rising towards each other, and meeting at an angle; the young one all the while uttering such a little quick note of gratitude and complacency, that a person must have paid very little regard to the wonders of nature that has not often remarked this feat."

Martins also feed their young flying, but not so commonly as Swallows; and the action is performed so swiftly that it usually escapes the notice of any one who is not a very quick observer.

A few years ago, when I was in Tangier, I was so fortunate as to have an opportunity of observing a pair of Wrynecks which were bringing up a young family in a hole in a tree, and frequently saw them busily engaged at an ants' nest taking in supplies for the family. The tip of the bird's tongue is very horny, and it uses this as an implement to stir up the ants and induce them to sally forth to defend their home. As they appear the bird gathers them wholesale into its mouth, where they are stuck together into a ball by means of the copious viscid saliva, exactly as in the case of the Swift, and the nutritious cake is then conveyed to the nest and dropped, I suppose, into the gaping mouths of the young Wrynecks.

These birds, which are slightly larger than a Sparrow, nest in some parts of England, where they arrive a few days before the Cuckoo and on that account are occasionally known as 'the Cuckoo's mate.' But as the hollow trees in our orchards, where they love to make their home, become fewer, the birds become rarer year by year, and they are now seen far less frequently than was the case fifty years ago. They are called Wryneck, or in some places 'Snake-bird,' because they have a wonderful way of twisting and writhing their head and neck, which is especially noticeable when one of the birds is caught and held by the feet. It is an easy matter to capture them while in the nesting-hole, and they would no doubt be molested more frequently than is actually the case but for the threaten-

FEEDING THE CHICKS

ing hiss with which they greet an intruder. Yet another snake-like characteristic of these curious birds is the rapidity with which the tongue is darted out when they are collecting insects.

Amongst Wrynecks both parents take a share in feeding the chicks, but with many species, such as the Skylark, the hen-bird alone performs this duty.

When young Skylarks are almost ready to leave the nest their mother feeds them about four times in every hour. Her return is heralded by a gentle twitter as she hovers above them for a few moments, " like a toy-bird suspended on the end of a bit of elastic," as Mr. Kearton happily describes her attitude at this time. The youngsters answer the call by shooting up their heads and opening wide their yellow mouths, whereupon the mother alights and gives one of them the worm she holds in her bill, after which, like a conjurer, she produces from somewhere at the back of her throat more worms and feeds the little ones in turn. The father's duty appears to consist merely in providing incidental music during and between the courses.

It is easy to observe the way in which a brood of callow nestlings respond to their parents' invitation to be fed, by paying a visit to a nest of young Thrushes, Hedge-Sparrows, or other common species, and imitating the sound made by the old birds. It need not be a particularly good imitation; the young birds are not fastidious, and are pretty sure to answer promptly by stretching their necks and gaping widely in anticipatiou of a meal. In many cases it is possible to get the same result by gently tapping the side of the nest or the twig on which it is supported, producing a swaying or vibration such as would be caused by a bird alighting. This can be repeated often, the chicks instinctively responding with a regularity which is ludicrously suggestive of the working of a mechanical toy when the spring is pressed. If, however, one of the old birds is anywhere about, uttering the alarm note, you will probably whistle or chirp or tap in vain, for the youngsters will cower down in the nest and remain still until you go away

FEEDING THE CHICKS

and they are assured by their anxious parent that the danger is past.

Most of the insect-eaters either drop the food into the mouths of their young or place it well back in their throats. The Nightjar, however, whose diet consists chiefly of moths and cockchafers, feeds its callow nestlings from the crop after the manner of Pigeons, but with this difference, that whereas the Pigeon takes the bill of the squab within its own, the Nightjar adopts the opposite plan and places its own bill in that of its young. In both cases there is the same jerking, up-and-down movement as the food is transferred from one to the other.

The Birds-of-Prey, on account of the nature of their food, feed their chicks less frequently than the birds we have hitherto mentioned. They bring in their supplies in bulk, consequently the young have substantial meals at longer intervals rather than a series of small courses spread over the whole day. Many of them carefully prepare the game before giving it to the young birds to eat. In Montana, for example, it has been noticed that the Golden Eagle always decapitates any small animals which it brings to the brood, but in the case of feathered prey, in which the skull is not so hard and unmanageable, the head is left on. Hares are *plucked*—a method of preparing this kind of game for the table which we usually only associate with the ancient story of the inexperienced cook. An Eagle's larder is kept well filled, for portions of dead animals are nearly always to be seen around the margins of the eyrie, and the young grow up literally 'in the midst of plenty.'

Reference to the Eagle's larder brings to mind the curious larder of the Red-backed Shrike (*Lanius collurio*), one of the summer visitors to England and the south of Scotland, better known by its popular name of 'Butcher-bird.' Its nest is usually placed high in a thorn bush, and on the surrounding thorns the bird impales the prey which it captures. Though considerably smaller than a Thrush it is very bold, and will even attack and kill other small birds, though the greater part

THE BUTCHER-BIRD'S LARDER

The Butcher-bird impales its prey on thorns, and the remains of many victims may often be seen on a favourite thorn-bush. The "larder" represented in the picture contains a beetle, a lizard, a young Blackbird, a Blue Titmouse, and a Hedge-Sparrow.

FEEDING THE CHICKS

of its food consists of large insects which it catches, after the manner of a Flycatcher, by making quick dashes from the twig where it sits perched and watchful. It kills even when its appetite for food is satisfied, and hangs up its victims for future consumption, dragging them on to the sharp thorns with its feet and strong bill, which is hooked and notched like that of a Bird-of-Prey. A strange variety of game is sometimes collected in the 'larder'; in one instance the bird had hung up a lizard, a dor-beetle, a Hedge-Sparrow, a young Blackbird, and a Blue Tit. Small frogs, mice, and humble-bees are amongst the other animals occasionally found there.

That charming little bird, the Dabchick, is remarkably careful about its children's diet. During the first fortnight of their life this consists mainly of fresh-water shrimps and such-like delicacies. The mother exercises careful supervision over the meals; if a fragment of food appears to be too solid for the little ones, she bites and crushes it in her bill to make it softer before giving it to them; if, having given it to them, it seems after all rather too large for them to manage, she promptly takes it away again. The Eider-Duck also carefully prepares the nursery dinner. Taking her brood of ducklings to a spot where edible mussels cover the rocks at low-water mark, she gathers as many as the family meal requires and, choosing the smallest, breaks the shells and lays the contents before her children.

Of the fish-eaters by far the greater number bring home the food in their gullet, though the noblest of them all, the Sea-Eagle, always carries its prey in its claws, and often brings to its young fish which are still alive. In Hungary, Prince Rudolph saw a Sea-Eagle flying home with a fish in each claw: on arriving at the nest it threw one of them to its young, and the other it took to a branch for its own supper.

Herons, Gannets, Cormorants, Petrels, Pelicans, and a host of other species, all carry the fish in their gullet, and allow the young to help themselves. Morning and evening the Heron

FEEDING THE CHICKS

flies home heavily from its fishing with laden crop, alights at the top of the tree, flaps its wings to recover its balance, and descends to the nest. The young, one after another, then put their beaks into their parent's and take the food—consisting not only of fish, but of frogs, small reptiles, shell-fish, and even young water-fowl—to an accompaniment of hoarse squeaks. The Brown Pelicans also feed their brood morning and evening. In the case of these birds, as in the Cormorants and others, the head and neck of the young are thrust far down into the parent's gullet in a way that is unpleasantly suggestive of possible cannibalism on the part of the old bird! It looks a most uncomfortable attitude for both parties, but they appear to derive much satisfaction from the operation.

In these and many other instances the young are fed at first on food which has already been partially digested, and are only gradually weaned to a more solid diet of fresh fish. The Gannet in its earliest days is nourished on a kind of fish soup prepared in its parent's gullet and stomach, and introduced a little at a time into the young bird's throat. The Petrels, which have such an unpleasant habit of bombarding any one who approaches them too closely when they are on the nest with a jet of evil-smelling oil, the odour of which clings to clothing for days afterwards, feed their young on the same unattractive fluid.

Even young birds have been known to submit to having their crops emptied by another nestling. Audubon has a story of two young Darters or Snake-birds—the species whose fishing is described in another chapter—which were kept in a cage, and relates that the smaller of the two when hungry worried his brother so persistently that at last the latter allowed him to put his head right down his throat and steal the fish which he had previously swallowed.

Chicks that grow quickly have prodigious appetites. The experience of a member of the *Discovery* Expedition, who attempted to bring home two baby Emperor Penguins from the

FEEDING THE CHICKS

Antarctic, is an amusing illustration of this. The little birds were very exacting, and made a great hullabaloo when they considered that meal-times had arrived. They were fed at first on crustaceans and afterwards on seal-meat, both of which had to be chewed up for them by their nurse.

This was no light occupation, for Captain Scott says that from the beginning they had to be regarded as small tanks, and that when they grew bigger they seemed to be bottomless caverns into which any quantity of food could be dropped without making much appreciable difference. After a while they began to disapprove of the long interval between supper and breakfast, and "used to go off like alarm clocks" in the middle of the night. Their nurse had then to get out of his warm bed—we may mention that he had from the first handed over his sleeping-jacket to his charges to protect them from the cold—and give them a meal: which meant that he had to chew seal-meat for them until they were satisfied, when their little heads would sink upon their distended bodies and they would sleep again until breakfast-time.

In a former chapter I mentioned that Ostrich eggs are often found scattered about the ground in the neighbourhood of the nest. It is said that when the young are hatched these scattered eggs are made use of by the parent birds as a sort of infant-food for their chicks; and that may well be so, for the shells are so thick that the contents keep perfectly fresh for several weeks.

Such, then, is the devotion of birds in appeasing the hunger of their little ones. It is only when they have been demoralised by domestication that they occasionally lapse into selfish conduct and allow their own greed to get the better of parental affection. For example, some years ago a Duck on the Long Water in Kensington Gardens used to seize her ducklings by the neck and hold them under the water until she was herself obliged to come to the surface to breathe, if they ventured to accept the crumbs thrown to them by a bystander.

CHAPTER V

DEFENCE OF HOME AND FAMILY

Change of character in breeding season—Courage and endurance—Braving cold, water, fire, famine, etc.—Intimidation—Strategy: the wiles of a Woodchuck—Attitude of an angry bird—Animals attacked by nesting birds: cats, dogs, pigs—Birds-of-Prey—Courage of Owls—The redoubtable King-bird—'Bonxies' and bonneting—An unpleasant habit—One of Nature's comedians.

AT the season of the year when they are chiefly occupied with family cares, birds not only put on braver attire, but change their character in harmony with the alteration in their plumage. The difference in the plumage, however, may in some cases be so slight as to pass almost unnoticed; but the contrast between the behaviour of a bird which has a home to defend and the same bird at other times is usually very remarkable indeed. However timid and spiritless it may have been, however ready to take to flight on the slightest alarm, it becomes pugnacious, aggressive, and often almost reckless in its courage. The Hen which, a few weeks before, ran fluttering and clucking across the farmyard pursued by a puppy, will not only stand her ground when she has a helpless brood to defend, but will fly in the face of any dog that dares to come near her precious charge. In many species it is the male bird who shows most devotion to the little ones and he may be no less determined in defence of his mate when she is sitting on the nest—or perhaps it is the nest he is thinking of rather than his partner; in any case, the result is the same.

The way in which birds protect their nurseries or little ones

DEFENCE OF HOME AND FAMILY

varies in different species; threats, force, and strategy all play their part, and may all be adopted by the same bird at different times, though usually we find that each species has its own particular method or combination of methods from the practice of which it rarely departs.

Devotion to its eggs, mate, or young is sometimes so overwhelming that a bird becomes entirely oblivious to its own safety. That famous naturalist, Thomas Edward—whose books you should read if you have not already done so—relates how, when crossing the Clasmauch on his way to Huntly after a heavy snowstorm which had compelled the Plovers and Wild Ducks to abandon their nests, he came upon one of the latter birds skulking, as he thought, beside a tuft of rushes. On approaching, however, he saw that she was dead, and there, beneath her lifeless body, was a nest with eleven eggs, each of which contained a young bird. It was evident that the poor Duck had died, half suffocated and half frozen, in the effort to protect her nest from the heavy fall of snow. That is an instance of passive endurance carried to the utmost limit; for the sake of their young or mate, however, birds exhibit active daring in no less a degree. We will take one or two homely instances of this.

Everybody knows that a Hen is a most devoted mother, and we shall have something more to say on this subject presently. In the farmyard her devotion results occasionally in some very curious situations, because not infrequently she is given a sitting of Duck's eggs to brood over, and when they are hatched the habits of her strange family are a terrible puzzle to her, and the source of much anxiety. This is especially the case when the whole brood, in spite of all her protests and her excited clucking, take to the water and swim beyond her reach, leaving her in a state of comical alarm on the edge of the pond. A case is recorded, however, of a Hen whose anxiety so far overcame her fear that she actually leapt into the pond in pursuit of her rebellious foster-children, and

DEFENCE OF HOME AND FAMILY

managed to swim to the other side—a distance of twenty feet.

Few birds are more cautious or more knowing than old Rooks and Crows, and to approach them openly within gunshot, if you are carrying a gun, is almost impossible—so difficult, indeed, that there is a tradition to the effect that they can smell powder! They have at all events learnt to distinguish a gun from a stick, for while they regard the latter with indifference, they take care to keep just beyond range of firearms. Yet even the wily Carrion-Crow falls a victim to parental affection. Mr. Cornish tells us that in the nesting-season he used to organise evening 'drives' of Crows in order to try to reduce their numbers before their destructive tendencies were further stimulated by the possession of ravenous families. On such an occasion, as soon as a shot was fired, one of the old birds came hurrying home to the nest to see what was happening, and immediately fell to the guns. A moment afterwards the other bird was seen, in the dim twilight, to descend straight on to the eggs, with the same fatal result.

This recalls the devotion of the Raven—made famous by Gilbert White's description—which had its nest in Losel's wood, at Selborne. We will give the story in his own words: "In the centre of this grove there stood an oak, which, though shapely and tall on the whole, bulged out into a large excrescence about the middle of the stem. On this a pair of ravens had fixed their residence for such a series of years, that the oak was distinguished by the title of the Raven-tree. Many were the attempts of the neighbouring youths to get at this eyry: the difficulty whetted their inclinations, and each was ambitious of surmounting the arduous task. But when they arrived at the swelling, it jutted out so in their way, and was so far beyond their grasp, that the most daring lads were awed, and acknowledged the undertaking to be too hazardous.

"So the ravens built on, nest upon nest, in perfect security, till the fatal day arrived in which the wood was to be levelled.

DEFENCE OF HOME AND FAMILY

It was in the month of February, when those birds usually sit. The saw was applied to the butt, the wedges were inserted into the opening, the woods echoed to the heavy blows of the beetle or mallet, the tree nodded to its fall; but still the dam sat on. At last, when it gave way, the bird was flung from her nest; and, though her parental affection deserved a better fate, was whipped down by the twigs, which brought her dead to the ground."

Amongst wild birds it is well known that the larger kinds exhibit most shyness at the approach of man; contrary to what one unacquainted with their habits might expect, the smaller the bird, the greater its fearlessness. If we bear this in mind it is not very surprising to find that some of the smaller species will endure a considerable amount of close observation when on the nest without taking to flight: we might easily give numerous examples, but one will suffice. Many years ago, a nest which had been built by a pair of Martins under the eaves of a house at Sutton was partially destroyed, as such nests often are, by a violent thunderstorm, and two little, unfledged birds fell to the ground. The owner of the house saw that they were apparently uninjured and considered what could be done to repair the damage. A ladder was brought to the spot and a piece of board was nailed up under the nest, which was then mended very carefully with clay. A little cotton-wool was put in to make good the damaged lining, and the young birds were replaced in the nest. Now all these operations necessarily caused a great deal of disturbance, yet during the whole time the parent bird never left the uninjured portion of the nest, but remained sitting there quietly until the work was finished, when, as if overcome by thankfulness for the kindness she had received, she flew around chirping cheerfully for several minutes.[1]

While birds which have discovered the advantages that houses and other buildings afford them as a nesting-site enjoy many benefits from their association with man, they have also

[1] Sterland's *Birds of Sherwood Forest*.

DEFENCE OF HOME AND FAMILY

to encounter the dangers of civilisation—dangers to which they are not exposed, or at all events but rarely, away from human habitations. One of these is the danger of fire, from which, for helpless nestlings, there is no hope of escape. The conduct of the parent birds in such circumstances amounts in many recorded instances to absolute self-sacrifice. We know that in Germany and elsewhere the bird which has most conspicuously attached itself to human dwellings is the White Stork, and a box or an old cart-wheel is frequently placed for its accommodation on roof or chimney by the householder. The bird is regarded as the type of a devoted parent; and so indeed it is, as the following instance goes to prove. At Neuendorf, in Prussia, a barn on which a pair of Storks had for years brought up a family was struck by lightning. The nest, a great heap of sticks big enough to make a good bonfire, at once burst into flames, but instead of flying to a place of safety, as she might have done, the mother Stork brooded over her helpless, screaming nestlings as if to protect them, and she and they together died amidst the flames. If you have read *A Tramp Abroad* by Mark Twain you may remember that he quotes in the Appendix an account of a similar incident which was related in a Mannheim journal.

Turning again to the smaller birds, American Chimney Swifts (*Chætura pelagica*) have on more than one occasion been seen to enter chimneys, where their nests were situated, when the house was on fire and the roof surrounded by flames. These birds have also been known to show their attachment to their young in a way which is somewhat unusual amongst birds which migrate, for it has often been remarked that great numbers of the young of such birds perish every year because the belated broods are not ready to leave the nest when the time comes for their parents to join the rest of their kind in their long flight to winter quarters, and as the migratory is usually even more powerful than the parental instinct, the young are left behind to starve.

DEFENCE OF HOME AND FAMILY

Some years ago, however, a writer in *Forest and Stream* recorded how, a month after the Swifts had departed, he heard the familiar twitter of these birds in his chimney, and on taking down the fire board, found a young Swift attached by a horsehair to a fallen nest. The mother bird entered the chimney and waited quietly while the thread was cut and the prisoner set at liberty. In about an hour the young one got the use of its legs and very quickly learnt to fly, so that at length the two birds were able to start in company on their lonely journey to a warmer climate. The parent had in this instance chosen to remain behind with her young one when all the rest of her companions were leaving the country, and had it not been for the timely assistance which they received both birds would no doubt have died of hunger, for insect food was already scarce.

We will now consider some of the means by which birds attempt to defend their young from hostile intruders. In the first place, then, many kinds try to ward off attack by threats, that is to say, by making themselves look as dangerous as they can, and by uttering strange sounds which no doubt often result in frightening away the enemy. "Nightingales," says Gilbert White, " when their young first come abroad, and are helpless, make a plaintive and a jarring noise: and also a snapping or cracking, pursuing people along the hedges as they walk: these last sounds seem intended for menace and defiance." A method which is much practised by birds which make their nests in holes in trees is to hiss like a snake—an effective procedure which has often prevented a nest from being plundered, for who would willingly put his hand into a dark hole which apparently is the home of a brood of young snakes? The Wryneck and the Nuthatch both adopt this plan.

The latter bird often nests in the deserted hole of a Woodpecker, taking care to plaster up the entrance until there is no room for the much larger Woodpecker to enter the cavity. If it be disturbed when occupying this stronghold, it fights

DEFENCE OF HOME AND FAMILY

most vigorously, striking with wings and bill, and hissing at the same time in a very terrible manner.

While discussing birds which nest in holes in trees, and the way in which they behave when they are surprised while on the nest, it may not be out of place to relate a little episode in the life of a family of California Screech-Owls (*Scops asio bendirei*) whose abode was a hole which had been made by Woodpeckers in a cottonwood tree. The nest was discovered by Mr. Gault, who found, on inserting his hand, that it was occupied by the parent bird and four nestlings about ten days old. As the mother bird was seized and forcibly removed from her home, she grasped one of the young family in her talons, and this in its turn took hold of another, and so on, with the result that in their efforts to resist eviction, they formed a continuous living chain of Owls which presented a very ludicrous sight as it came dangling out of the hole.

The behaviour of Woodpeckers themselves is by no means devoid of interest. There is a species called the Pileated Woodpecker (*Picus pileatus*), but more popularly known, in common with the Red-bellied Woodpecker, as the 'Woodchuck,' which is found over almost the whole of North America. This splendid bird, which is unfortunately now becoming rare, is a very powerful and artistic workman, and it is said that when it is cutting a hole in a tree-trunk for the purpose of making its nest, it often removes the traces of its presence by carrying away the chips and scattering them at a distance. Those who have read *The Romance of Animal Arts and Crafts* will remember that some of the carpenter-ants take similar precautions against discovery. According to Dr. Ralph, the Woodchuck can, on occasion, act in a still more remarkable manner with the object of protecting its home. One spring, in Florida, Dr. Ralph found a nest excavated in a dead cypress tree, and rapped on the trunk to ascertain whether the bird was at home. The Woodchuck immediately put his head out of the hole and dropped some chips, whereupon the doctor con-

DEFENCE OF HOME AND FAMILY

cluded that the carpentry was still going on and that the nest was unfinished. As the same thing occurred on several subsequent visits he decided to examine the nest in any case, and on doing so he was surprised to find that it contained a brood of young birds, very nearly full grown! The chips, then, had apparently been thrown out by the old bird with the object of deceiving him—of hoodwinking the intruder, that is to say, concerning the advanced state of family life.

In America, where Cuckoos take a more serious view of thei responsibility than does the light-hearted vagabond with which we are familiar in England, the shyest amongst them become bold when their nest and eggs are in danger. The Yellow-billed Cuckoo, for instance, when on the nest will often raise its feathers until they stand out at right angles to its body, "like quills upon the fretful porcupine," not from fear—for a bird that is alarmed depresses its feathers close to the body and makes itself as small as possible—but from anger. This Cuckoo is at ordinary times a timid bird, but it has been known to fly fiercely at an intruder upon the privacy of its home. In such circumstances, and especially if there are young ones in danger, birds will often boldly attack their most inveterate enemies. A Blackbird has been seen to attack a cat which had caught one of its fledglings, and by pecking vigorously and beating her wings in the cat's face, to compel her to release her prey. The Game-birds are as plucky as any in this respect, and most sportsmen are aware that a Partridge will often 'stand up to,' and even drive off, a terrier. In America the Ruffed Grouse is equally plucky. Captain Bendire saw a hen of this species attack an Indian dog and absolutely make him turn tail and slink away, by sheer force of character and reckless fierceness. Every feather on her body stood on end, and she hissed like an angry cat, pecking the dog's head and legs and moving to the attack with such agility that he was glad to make an ignominious escape from her fury.

Just as much determination is shown by the male bird in de-

DEFENCE OF HOME AND FAMILY

fence of his mate when sitting. Gilbert White recorded in his diary, March 21st, 1783, "My Goose sits, while the Gander with vast assiduity keeps guard, and takes the fiercest sow by the ear, and leads her away crying." So it is, too, with wild Geese. The male Grey-Lag faithfully watches beside the Goose and guards her all the time she is sitting, and the male Canada Goose will resolutely face the greatest peril while he urges his wife to fly from the nest, standing his ground bravely until she has reached a place of safety, when he also takes to flight.

Many are the tales which have been told concerning the dangers which beset the man who dares to attempt to rob the Golden Eagle of its young or eggs: stories of the majestic birds swooping down in righteous anger and fiercely attacking the robber as he hangs perilously suspended from a slender rope over the face of the rocky cliff where the birds have their eyrie, or clings precariously to a narrow ledge. It is very doubtful, however, whether there is any foundation whatever for these adventurous tales, for Golden Eagles, though courageous enough, appear to possess but little parental affection, and I have never come across a really reliable account of these birds making the least attempt to defend their young. Usually they fly away and either disappear from sight altogether or watch the robbery from afar. All Birds-of-Prey do not behave in this callous fashion, however; some of them have a way of swooping down close to the head of any person who approaches their nest and uttering ear-piercing shrieks, but they seldom actually make an attack.

There are, however, exceptions, and it is well for the intruder to be prepared for emergencies. Robbing an Osprey's nest is a dangerous proceeding, and some of the Goshawks are particularly vigorous in their attacks on any one who ventures to climb towards the nest. Usually the female alone is the defender of the home, but occasionally, as with the Sharp-shinned Hawk, male and female join forces and buffet the egg-collector rather severely.

What might be the result of one of the larger Birds-of-Prey coming down upon a man's head from a great height it is

DEFENDING THE HOME

"My goose sits, while the gander with vast assiduity keeps guard, and takes the fiercest sow by the ear, and leads her away crying."

DEFENCE OF HOME AND FAMILY

difficult to say, but if one may judge by comparison with the impression produced by an Owl, it would be far from agreeable, as the following incident, which occurred in the neighbourhood of my own home, will show. One evening a gentleman was walking through a wood beside a small lake when a young Owl fluttered past him and alighted on the ground. Without difficulty he caught the little bird under his cap; but just at that moment a strange thing happened. As described by himself, he was apparently "struck on the head by a brick," and was so disconcerted that his captive was allowed to escape; but what had really occurred was that one of the old birds had come to the rescue of her young, and had very successfully pounced down upon the head of its captor.

The Owls, indeed, are a brave family, and if it would not be too tedious we might, I think, without much difficulty, show that scarcely a single species is devoid of courage. We must be content with one more instance before passing on to a different aspect of defence. In this case a dog and his master were passing within a short distance of the spot where a pair of Short-eared Owls (*Asio accipitrinus*) had their nest. Both birds set to work to drive away the dog by swooping upon him from side to side and striking him on the back with their wings. He was not accustomed to birds conducting themselves so boldly, and he beat a hasty retreat, pursued for some distance by the angry Owls, who then turned their attention to the dog's master and endeavoured to drive him away also by swooping very close to him and snapping their beaks.

So far we have been mainly concerned with the various methods of defence adopted by birds, great and small, against man and mammals. But there are other enemies, of their own race, to be encountered, and here again we constantly meet with instances of impetuous daring. The most remarkable of them all is the behaviour of the King-bird (*Tyrannus tyrannus*), one of the best-known birds of the United States, during the summer months. He is not a large bird—rather smaller,

DEFENCE OF HOME AND FAMILY

indeed, than our English Blackbird; nor is he particularly showy, though his black back and white front and his little flame-coloured crest, which in repose lies half hidden, are handsome enough, when added to his bold and confident bearing, to give him a very gentlemanly and even noble appearance. As for song, his shrill twitter is hardly worthy of the name. What is it, then, that makes this little bird so very remarkable? It is this: from the moment the foundation twigs of his big, compact nest are laid, until the day when his young family are able to fight their own battles, he divides his time between feeding and entertaining his mate and little ones and giving battle, from morn till night, to every bird that ventures anywhere near his precious nest. His impetuosity is irresistible, and he attacks every intruder without discrimination. Even cats quickly learn to shun the neighbourhood.

"In the months of May, June, and part of July," says Wilson, "his life is one continued scene of broils and battles; in which, however, he generally comes off conqueror. Hawks and Crows, the Bald Eagle and the great Black Eagle, all equally dread a rencontre with this dauntless little champion, who, as soon as he perceives one of these last approaching, launches into the air to meet him, mounts to a considerable height above him, and darts down on his back, sometimes fixing there to the great annoyance of his sovereign, who, if no convenient retreat or resting-place be near, endeavours by various evolutions to rid himself of his merciless adversary. But the King-bird is not so easily dismounted—he teases the Eagle incessantly, sweeps upon him from right to left, remounts, that he may descend on his back with the greater violence; all the while keeping up a shrill and rapid twittering; and continning the attack sometimes for more than a mile, till he is relieved by some other of his tribe equally eager for the contest." There appear to be but three birds which are able to contend with this champion: one is the Purple Martin (*Progne*), whose marvellous powers of flight enable him to escape; another

DEFENCE OF HOME AND FAMILY

is the Red-headed Woodpecker, who greatly irritates the little tyrant by his skill in dodging him round the perch where he has taken refuge, and apparently much enjoys the game; and the third is a little Humming-bird, which simply defies this conqueror of Eagles, and is said very often to come off best!

Even an ordinary farmyard Hen has been seen attacking a Hawk, which was on the point of carrying off one of her chickens, with such force as to throw the marauder on its back, whereupon she continued the fight with feet and bill so effectively that Audubon, who relates this story, was able to secure the Hawk before it could escape from the infuriated mother.

Some of the Ducks are hardly less devoted, but it must be admitted that the drakes *are*, for they are constantly in the habit of shirking their responsibilities and leaving all the care of the brood to their mates. If disturbed when taking her family for a swim, the Eider-Duck covers their retreat by beating the water with her wings and so raising a screen of spray all around, while, by means of a peculiar sound, she urges her little ones to dive. If hard pressed, she will spring out of the water to attack the enemy; but a favourite device is to feign lameness, and so entice the intruder to follow her while her chicks make good their escape. This is a method which is practised by birds of many species, and we shall have to return to it later. Gulls are amongst the worst enemies of the Eider ducklings, and both Brehm and Audubon have noticed that two Ducks sometimes very prudently join forces for the more effectual guarding of their young, which are then seldom assailed.

As for the Gulls themselves, they make a terrible fuss when a man visits their nesting-colony; and their near relatives the strong, piratical Skuas, or 'Bonxies,' as they are called in the Shetlands, are in the habit, when *their* breeding-grounds are invaded, of swooping down upon the visitor's head from a height of about two hundred feet. As the birds get near their speed is terrific; just before reaching the intruder they drop their feet, and strike in passing, often knocking the cap off the

DEFENCE OF HOME AND FAMILY

head. According to Graba, bird-catchers sometimes hold knives above their caps, with the result that the impetuous birds occasionally impale themselves on the blade in their violent swoop. Both male and female join in the attack; the swoop is invariably made from behind, and directly after striking the bird rises gracefully on outstretched wings and wheels round to prepare for another attack. In the Antarctic the Skuas, when disturbed while guarding their fluffy little slate-coloured chicks, wheel round and swoop down in a similar manner, with wild cries; but Captain Scott says that he does not think any member of his party was ever actually struck, for at the last moment the birds used to turn aside. They often passed so near, however, that the men were brushed by their wings; and their tactics were decidedly alarming, for the Skua is a big heavy bird with a large ugly bill, and quite able, if it were just a little more courageous, to give a lot of trouble.

The Tropic-Bird (*Phaethon*), or 'Boatswain' as sailors call it, adopts similar tactics towards man. Leguat, who named this bird *Straw-Tail* on account of the peculiar projecting middle feathers, says: "These Birds made a pleasant War upon us, or rather upon our Bonnets; they often came behind us, and caught 'em off our Heads before we were aware of it: this they did so frequently that we were forced to carry Sticks in our hands to defend our selves. We prevented them sometimes, when we discovered them by their shadow before us: we then struck them in the Moment they were about to strike us. We cou'd never find out of what use the Bonnets were to them, nor what they did with those they took from us"—from which we must evidently understand that, unlike the Bonxies, Leguat's Straw-Tails were not content with knocking off the sailors' bonnets, but carried them away. It is interesting to note that both Boatswain and Bonxie are thoroughgoing buccaneers, and we shall have something to say about their piratical habits in another chapter.

The Giant Petrel (*Ossifraga gigantea*), or 'Nelly' of sailors,

DEFENCE OF HOME AND FAMILY

has a more unpleasant way of repelling invaders. In the South Orkney Islands these birds, which are vultures in habit, form rookeries of about two hundred nests all within a small area, though not quite so close together as the nests in a Penguin rookery. Each nest consists of half a bushel of pebbles and measures two or three feet in diameter; on this heap of stones a pure white egg is deposited. In order to secure the egg, the bird has to be knocked off the nest, and it shows its resentment and does its best to protect its property by sitting down a yard or two away and ejecting the contents of its stomach at the intruder! The result is such that there is no doubt whatever that the old sealers were amply justified in giving to these birds the uncomplimentary name of 'Stinkers.'

A more sportsmanlike method of defence is adopted by the aristocracy of Antarctic avifauna, the Penguins.

Dr. Wilson, who accompanied Captain Scott on his voyage "furthest south," and whose interesting observations have added so greatly to our knowledge of the natural history of the Antarctic, writes concerning that comical creature the Adélie Penguin: "It would require a cinematograph to do justice to the peculiarities of the Penguin. . . . When annoyed in any way, the cock bird ranges up in front of his wife, his eyes flashing anger, his feathers erect in a ruffle round his head, and his language unfit for publication. He stands there for a minute or two breathing out threatenings and slaughter till his rage overpowers him, and putting his head down he makes a dash at one's legs and hails blows upon them with his flippers like bullets from a machine gun."

Enough instances have now been given to show that many birds, both great and small, will offer plucky resistance to an intruder whom they suspect of harbouring unfriendly intentions towards their family; but there is another kind of defence which is of peculiar interest, and which we must consider in the next chapter.

CHAPTER VI

MAKE-BELIEVE: A STUDY IN INSTINCT

Deceptive behaviour—The 'little brown bird'—Death-feigning—Lapwings and egg-gatherers—Wiles of the male bird and protective colouration of the eggs—Avosets and Stilts—Ducks and Drakes—Ostrich—Unkingly conduct of a King Vulture—Some artful dodgers—A cat's hunting—The paralysing effect of fear and the advantage which hunters take of it—Difference between death-feigning and the immobility of protectively coloured birds—The real 'possum—The popular idea of a 'shamming' bird—A true fairy-tale—Natural selection.

IN describing the various ways in which birds protect their young we have hitherto hardly referred to the strangest and most interesting of them all, but this is really an advantage, because if we consider it by itself we are more likely to come a little nearer to understanding what is a very puzzling question. Every sportsman and every naturalist is aware that when certain birds feel that their nests or young are in danger they behave in a very curious manner, fluttering or limping over the ground as though they were badly wounded and had the greatest difficulty in making good their retreat. The result of this strange behaviour is that the enemy is often completely deceived by their actions and is lured on in pursuit, for it seems impossible that the bird can escape as it struggles wildly only a few yards ahead, apparently almost exhausted by its efforts. Time after time it is almost within reach, and to all appearance it cannot possibly elude capture much longer; but somehow it always manages to keep just out of reach until, seeming suddenly to recover, it flies rapidly away and the chase becomes hopeless. Many of the Game-birds are most skilful performers of this little comedy, but the same method is re-

MAKE-BELIEVE: A STUDY IN INSTINCT

sorted to by a great variety of birds, from the little Warbler to the mighty Ostrich; Lapwings, Plovers, Rails, Avosets, Ducks, Pigeons, Pipits, and Buntings are all adepts in the practice. It is difficult even for those who are aware of their habits not to be deceived, while dogs are easy dupes and never fail to be led away by the manœuvre. When the chase is over and the bird has flown, the pursuer is usually far away from the nest, and if there be young ones they have had ample time to scatter in all directions and find secure hiding-places where it is almost hopeless to try to find them.

Our common Partridge is one of the best known exponents of this curious trick. Its devotion to its eggs and young is familiar to all dwellers in the country, but no amount of familiarity can diminish the interest which is excited by its wonderful devices. The rapidity with which a brood of young Partridges will make good their retreat while the parents distract attention by their antics, and the completeness with which they disappear from sight, have frequently been described.

Sterland, in his book on the birds of Sherwood Forest, says: "I once came suddenly on a brood of young ones, who could not have been more than a day or two old; they were accompanied by both old ones, and were busily feeding on an anthill in the midst of the moss and heather. On my unexpected appearance, the cock bird tumbled off on one side and the hen on the other, with well-feigned lameness. Out of curiosity I threw myself on the ground and tried to secure some of the young ones; but, to my surprise, it was in vain. A few seconds before, there were ten or a dozen of them in a spot scarcely larger than my hat, but before I was down on my knees, they were dispersed in all directions amongst the surrounding heather, and I failed to capture one of them. I could not help admiring the instinct which prompted these tiny things to such instant and energetic action, for it could not have been acquired by imitation or experience."

Some birds carry the deception a step further and simulate

MAKE-BELIEVE: A STUDY IN INSTINCT

death, but this heroic measure is more often resorted to as a means of self-protection than for the purpose of assisting in the escape of the young. That is what we should expéct, because it is clearly a greater advantage to the brood if the enemy can be induced to leave the neighbourhood, and that can best be done by enticing him in the way we are now considering. Still, 'death-feigning,' as it is usually called, is sometimes practised by anxious parents, and Audubon observed it in the case of the American Woodcock (*Scolopax minor*), who "regardless of her own danger ... lay herself down in the middle of a road as if she were dead, while her little ones, five in number, were endeavouring on feeble legs to escape from a pack of naughty boys." We are not told whether the five young Woodcocks got away from their tormentors, but no doubt the weaker side found a good friend in the kindly naturalist. Few of us, however, have an opportunity of witnessing quite such a stirring drama in bird-life; yet the everyday incidents are hardly less interesting, and some of the most familiar birds are always ready to 'play the game' at the proper season of the year.

Wherever there are broad, barren pastures, ploughed fields, or moorland—almost anywhere, in fact, if only the ground be open enough—we may hear the wild, wailing cry and see the graceful flight of that most beautiful and picturesque of our common birds—the Lapwing, or Pewit. Perhaps there is no bird of blameless life—from our point of view—which is so greatly persecuted as this. Its handsome livery, which at a distance appears to be of black and white in about equal proportions, but the dark parts of which are really a beautiful green gleaming with purple and enlivened with bronzed reflections, makes it an easy mark for the gun; while its eggs—commonly known as 'Plovers' eggs'—are taken by thousands to be sold for the table. Not that all the so-called Plovers' eggs of the market are really what they pretend to be: many of them are those of the Black-headed Gull, or of some of the

MAKE-BELIEVE: A STUDY IN INSTINCT

Terns, which are rather like Lapwings' eggs in appearance, and can hardly be distinguished from them in flavour except by people with a very delicate sense of taste. It is commonly believed that Rooks also contribute to the supply of 'Plovers' eggs,' but that is an absurd notion, for there is not the slightest resemblance between the shells of the two kinds, and it would be impossible to mistake one for the other.

Most of the eggs sold as Plovers', however, are those of the Pewit, and the birds' domestic arrangements suffer in consequence very severely at the hands of man. There is no doubt that they would be still more interfered with if the male bird were not so skilled in the art of deception during the nesting season. Probably most schoolboys are aware how difficult it is for a novice to discover a Pewit's nest in a large field. Here and there a bird is seen flapping in easy, irregular curves over the ground, uttering its unmistakable cry, and you watch carefully to ascertain in which spot its interest is centred: then you walk towards it. As you approach, the plaintive notes become more frequent, and the bird seems to be more and more distressed; it screams and complains, and falters in its flight; it dashes and tumbles frantically hither and thither, and you feel quite sure that the nest is within a few yards of you. But no—you decide that you were mistaken: you had misjudged the distance, and the nest must certainly be a little further on, for there is the bird in greater distress than ever; and surely it has hurt its wing? Why, it can hardly fly —see how it is tumbling over the ground! Ah, you nearly overtook it then, it only *just* managed to dash away! But the effort has exhausted it, and now it can scarcely control its movements in its desperate efforts to escape. Away over the ground it plunges and the pursuit becomes more exciting until—why, what is this? The bird has recovered and is flying easily— forty—fifty—a hundred yards away! Tired and breathless, you turn again to look for the nest, only to realise that, so far as you can remember, it was somewhere over there, on the

MAKE-BELIEVE: A STUDY IN INSTINCT

other side of the field, that you first noticed the bird. So you walk across, and to and fro, and look on this side and on that; but one bit of ground seems just as likely as another and no nest is visible anywhere: perhaps you were wrong after all, and the birds have no nest in that particular field.

Now that, or something like that, is what occurs when a novice turns aside from his path to look for Plovers' eggs; but let us watch a man who had had experience in collecting them for the market. He looks over the field and sees birds wheeling about, flashing black and white in the early sunlight, and he hears their complaining; but he does not heed them. His attention is directed to those other birds that rise silently and unobtrusively as he approaches, and he carefully notes the spot which each one leaves. He does not regard the frantic behaviour of the cock, but walks straight to the spot from which the hen has risen, looks narrowly around, and then, a few yards away, something attracts his attention.

Let us suppose we are by his side; very probably we see nothing at all except the rough ground and here and there, perhaps, a few scattered stones. But the egg-gatherer steps forward and stoops down; and *then* suddenly we see the nest and its precious contents, and we understand why we did not perceive it before. For the nest is nothing more than a slight hollow in the ground with perhaps a few bits of dry grass or other vegetation around its margin, and the four black-spotted olive eggs, lying with the pointed ends all together (in which position they occupy least space and are most easily covered by the sitting bird), are scarcely to be distinguished from their surroundings, unless one happens to be looking directly at them. So although the Lapwing entrusts its treasure to the bare, open ground, and although its plumage is so conspicuous, it is seldom that the nest is seen, except by the trained eye, owing to the 'protective colouration' of the eggs and, what we are now particularly concerned with, the wiles of the male bird in leading the intruder astray. Only the superior cunning of the pro-

Lapwing Leaving its Nest

When alarmed by the approach of an intruder the lapwing tries to divert attention from its eggs by dashing and tumbling about wildly, like a wounded bird, and is often successful in luring the enemy away from its treasures.

MAKE-BELIEVE: A STUDY IN INSTINCT

fessional collector enables him to walk straight up to one nest after another, and even to judge, from the behaviour of the hen, whether he will find the full number of eggs and whether the bird has begun to sit.

Other members of the same great group as the Woodcock and the Lapwing have their own peculiar methods of counterfeiting lameness. We will mention but two—those strange and interesting birds the Avoset and the Stilt. The Avoset (*Recurvirostra avocetta*) is a bird about as big as a Lapwing and is remarkable for possessing, in proportion to its size, one of the most slender of bills, which is curved like a cobbler's awl, with the point turned upwards. Of old time these birds were plentiful in certain parts of England, such as Romney Marsh and the fen district. In Norfolk and Suffolk people made puddings of their eggs, and their feathers were used for tying artificial flies for fishing. But though they still visit us occasionally they have long ceased to dwell with us, and none has been known to breed in this country for almost half a century. We learn, however, from the accounts of older naturalists, that when the female was frightened off her nest it was *she* who counterfeited lameness; and before passing on to the Stilt we may mention that it is likewise the hen who adopts this method of defence in the case of the pretty little American Ground-Dove, in the Southern States. Dr. Ralph says: "When one is driven from a nest containing eggs it will drop to the ground as if shot, and will then flutter around as if wounded, to try to draw the person disturbing it away from the nest, but, whether it succeeds or not, it will soon fly off." This little bird is more interesting in its ways than the majority of the Pigeons, which are not usually very entertaining, for when there are young in the nest it is very determined in its efforts, fluttering and tumbling and dashing around in the wildest manner until it appears wellnigh exhausted by the violence of its antics.

The Stilt (*Himantopus candidus*) is a much smaller bird than the Avoset, being in fact no larger than a Snipe, but it has extra-

MAKE-BELIEVE: A STUDY IN INSTINCT

ordinarily long legs—longer, in proportion, than those of any other species, not even excepting the Flamingo; on this account it is sometimes called the 'Longshanks,' or Long-legged Plover. Its home is on the muddy margin of pools and lakes, but it is only an occasional visitor to Great Britain.

When the hen-birds are sitting their partners roam over the marshes or wade in the pools, hunting for food about the surface of the water, but as soon as anybody approaches they all flock together and fly around, with their long legs trailing out behind, keeping up a continual yelping cry. Wilson says: "As they frequently alight on the bare marsh, they drop their wings, stand with their legs half bent, and trembling, as if unable to sustain the burden of their bodies. In this ridiculous posture they will sometimes stand for several minutes, uttering a curring sound, while from the corresponding quiverings of their wings and long legs, they seem to balance themselves with great difficulty. This singular manœuvre is, no doubt, intended to induce a belief that they may be easily caught, and so turn the attention of the person from the pursuit of their nests and young to themselves."

Amongst the Ducks the seeming lameness takes yet another form, as we should expect from their different build. If the fine, handsome, sturdy Sheld-ducks are disturbed when taking their young family to the water for a swim, they trail and limp along the ground as though they had all their lives suffered severely from rheumatism and could hardly put one foot before the other; then, when they have succeeded in their object of warding off the danger from their little ones, they hurriedly return to them and fuss over them like the devoted parents that they are.

A more familiar bird than the Sheld-duck in England is the ordinary Wild Duck. In his delightful book on *Wild England of To-day*, Mr. Cornish describes how a pair of Wild Drakes were flushed from a shallow ditch near the lake in Richmond Park. "Almost at the same moment a lame duck shuffled

MAKE-BELIEVE: A STUDY IN INSTINCT

distressfully from the same spot, and moved off slowly, with apparent difficulty, in a direction parallel to the lake. The counterfeit was so remarkable, that had we not caught a glimpse of a small black object dashing into the marsh which lay a few feet from the drain on the opposite side to the course taken by the duck, no suspicion as to the reality of her disablement would have occurred. Meanwhile, the old bird invited pursuit, lying down, as if unable to move further; and, resolved to see the end of so finished and courageous a piece of acting, we accepted the invitation and gave chase. For twenty yards or more the bird shuffled and stumbled through the rhododendron bushes, until she made for the lakeside, where the ground was more open. There, running fast, with her head up and discarding all pretence of lameness, for another twenty yards, she took wing, and flew slowly just before us, at about three feet from the ground, until she reached the limit of the enclosure, when, uttering a derisive quack, she rose quickly above the trees and flew out over the lake.

"Anxious to see the sequel to this beautiful instance of maternal affection, we hurried back to the little marsh where the ducklings were probably hidden, and, sheltered under a rhododendron bush, awaited the return of the . . . wild duck to her brood. In a few minutes she reappeared, flying swiftly in circles among the trees, and after satisfying herself that the danger was past, she alighted among some wild-currant bushes about thirty yards from the marsh. There she stood for a moment, still and listening, with head erect; and, seeing nothing to alarm her, ran bustling down to the drain. After realising that no harm had overtaken her brood on the spot where they had been surprised, she climbed the bank and tripped lightly into the marsh, where, in answer to her low quack, we soon heard the piping voices of the ducklings, which till then had remained motionless and invisible in the few yards of grass and rushes near. In a few seconds the whole

MAKE-BELIEVE: A STUDY IN INSTINCT

family were united, and we had the pleasure of seeing the old bird swim past at the head of an active fleet of eleven black-and-yellow ducklings, making for the centre of the marsh."

All these birds are habitually self-sacrificing—or at least appear to place themselves in considerable danger—for the sake of their young; but we occasionally find instances of similar conduct in species that are as a rule by no means so exemplary in their devotion. The Ostrich is one of these; when surprised by man in the company of its young, the parent Ostrich usually scuds off as fast as he can over the desert and leaves the chicks to shift for themselves.

On one occasion, however, Mr. Anderson and Mr. Galton came upon a pair of Ostriches which showed more affection for their young. As these gentlemen approached, the whole family took to flight in company, the mother leading, followed by her chicks, and the cock-bird bringing up the rear some distance away. The chicks were unable to cover the ground very quickly and the male soon discovered that they were being beaten in the race, so he deliberately slackened his pace and turned aside a little. The hunters, however, refused to be led away, so he increased his speed and with drooping wings began to rush at a tremendous pace round and round the pursuers, gradually decreasing his circle and coming nearer to them until he was within pistol-shot, when he suddenly dropped to the ground and seemed to be making desperate efforts to regain his feet. A shot had already been fired at him, and Mr. Anderson hurried towards him in the belief that he was disabled. In that opinion he was mistaken, however, for as soon as it appeared wise to retreat the bird rose to his feet and began to scud away in the opposite direction, while his family, who had in the meantime put a wide space between themselves and their pursuers, continued on their course uninjured.

We have given enough examples of the strange instinct which leads birds of many species to behave as if they were wounded or otherwise disabled, with the result that their enemies

MAKE-BELIEVE: A STUDY IN INSTINCT

are often lured away from the nest or young, which thus escape destruction: we have described the tumbling flight of the Partridge, the antics and distressed cries of the male Lapwing, the similar conduct of the hen Avoset; we have spoken of the attitudinising of the Stilt, the hobbling run of the Sheld-duck, the tactics of a Wild Duck, the frantic action of the American Ground-Dove, and the curious strategy of a male Ostrich; we have mentioned also how an American Woodcock went even further than any of these, and lay in the road as if dead, when its brood was in danger. It will be interesting now to consider how the death-feigning instinct serves birds for self-defence, and to try to understand the meaning of it all, if we can.

I remember seeing, many years ago, a young King Vulture which had recently arrived at the 'Zoo' from South America. He was a well-grown youngster, about as large as a Goose, but he was very shy and behaved in a most unkingly way in the presence of strangers, when he was being watched, for he used to crouch down, lay his head upon the ground, and remain quite still, like a dead bird. The North American Screech-Owl (*Scops asio*) of the Rocky Mountains also practises this deception. When the female is removed from her nest, she sometimes moans, snaps her bill, and shows fight; frequently, however, she does none of these things, but lies back perfectly motionless in the open hand with her eyes shut, to all appearance dead. If she be thrown up into the air while in this condition, she rights herself at once on the wing and alights on a neighbouring bough, where she stands crouching forward, with her ear-tufts turned back in a way that is suggestive of a bad-tempered horse, looking very spiteful and wicked.

We need not, however, go abroad for instances of death-feigning, for it is practised by a bird which is one of the commonest British species, although, owing to its stealthy habits, most people have never seen it. We refer to the Land-

MAKE-BELIEVE: A STUDY IN INSTINCT

Rail or Corncrake (*Crex pratensis*), whose curious, double, creaking cry, uttered as it skulks amongst the meadow grass, may be heard incessantly during the spring at almost all times of the day and night. Canon Atkinson has given an amusing account of the behaviour of this bird when captured, which we will quote. He says: "A gentleman's dog catches a land-rail and brings it to his master, unhurt, of course, as is the well-trained dog's way, but to all appearance perfectly dead. The dog lays the bird down at his master's feet, and he turns it over with his toe. It simply moves as it is moved, all its limbs limp. Continuing to regard it, however, the man sees an eye opened, and he takes it up. The 'artful dodger' is quite dead again in a moment, head hanging and dangling, limbs loose, and no sign of life anywhere. It is put in its captor's pocket, and, not liking the confinement, begins to struggle. When taken out, it is just as lifeless as before; but being put down on the ground and left undisturbed—the gentleman having stepped to one side, but continuing to watch—it lifts its head in a minute or so, and, seeing all apparently serene, it starts up on a sudden and 'cuts its lucky' with singular speed."

Now, is the bird really an "artful dodger," or is it so timid that it is terrified into insensibility—a second and perhaps a third time—as soon as it discovers on opening an eye that its enemy is still there? That is a question which we are not yet in a position to answer. The marsh-dwelling Water-Rail (*Rallus aquaticus*), also a skulker, can 'play 'possum' just as successfully, and Canon Atkinson's account goes on to say: "In the case of the water-rail, which came under my own observation, it was picked up on a snowy day by the most intimate of the friends of my youth and early manhood. He assumed that it was dazed with cold, and perhaps what we Yorkshire folks call 'hungered' as well. So he brought it home with him, and laid it on a foot-stool in front of the dining-room fire. Five minutes passed— ten were gone—and still the lifeless bird lay as it was put down,

MAKE-BELIEVE: A STUDY IN INSTINCT

dead to all seeming; only not stiff, as it ought to have been, if dead of cold as well as hunger. A few minutes later, my friend, who was very still, but yet with an eye to the bird, saw it—not lift its head, like the land-rail, and take a view, but—start off in a moment with no previous intimation of its purpose, and begin to career about the room with incredible rapidity. It never attempted to fly. Any other captive bird in its position would have made for the window at once, and beaten itself half to pieces against the glass. Not so the rail. With it, in its helter-skelter and most erratic course, it was anywhere rather than the window or the fire. Round the room, across the room, under the sofa, under the table, from corner to corner, steering itself perfectly, notwithstanding legs of chairs, legs of tables, the sofa-feet, footstools, or what not, on and on it careered; and it was not without some patience and many attempts that it was eventually secured."

Such a sudden change from death-like stillness to frenzied activity is what we should expect in an animal recovering from a swoon and finding itself in an alarming situation from which its sole desire is to escape at all costs, rather than the behaviour of a good actor bent on hoodwinking his audience until he sees a favourable opportunity of slipping away unobserved. Perhaps the bird was frightened out of its senses when first surprised in a weak condition brought on by hunger and cold, but was not so easily overcome by fright when its circulation had been restored in front of the warm fire, and had then sufficient presence of mind to take to its heels (it would be more correct to say, take to its *toes* in the case of a bird) and try to get away.

The question is, can a bird be so terrified as to be paralysed by fear? I think it can. From my college rooms I used to have many opportunities of watching a fine black tom-cat hunting Sparrows. Tom's favourite method was to lie concealed under a laurel bush beside the lawn and wait patiently until a Sparrow alighted within reach, and then to make a spring.

MAKE-BELIEVE: A STUDY IN INSTINCT

He was seldom successful, for he was getting old and, though still a fine figure of a cat, was rather stout and not so agile as a younger animal. But he never seemed to tire of his hunting, and in this he sometimes reminded me of those patient anglers who are quite content to sit the livelong day beside a stream whether they catch anything or nothing. But to return to our story: occasionally a Sparrow would hop about in a tantalising way just a little too far off for the hunter to risk a spring; he would then creep out from his hiding-place very stealthily in the hope of getting nearer unobserved. Very often, however, the Sparrow would catch sight of him before he was close enough to pounce upon it, and then I noticed that the bird was usually too terrified to fly away immediately—or at all events did not fly at once, as it no doubt would have done had it been able. Frequently there was quite a long pause before its little body sank close to the ground for the spring which helps the wings at the beginning of flight; and Tom, in spite of his years, was often the first to jump.

There can be little doubt that this momentary overwhelming sense of terror in birds, when they first catch sight of their deadly enemy at close quarters, gives the cat a great advantage in its hunting and enormously increases the number of victims. The so-called 'fascination' exercised by snakes over their prey is due to a similar cause; and certain other birds besides the Land-Rail and Water-Rail are affected in the same way by man. The fine Pileated Woodpecker (*Picus pileatus*), commonly known in North America, which is its native country, as the Logcock, is paralysed with fright if a man approaches unheard and makes suddenly as though to catch it. Not infrequently it falls to the ground as if dead without being touched, but when left to itself it quickly recovers and flies off with the utmost speed. On the pampas of the Argentine, in the Southern continent, Mr. Hudson tells us that the gauchos often capture the Black-necked Swan (*Cygnus nigricollis*) by frightening it. This is a large, handsome bird with a pure

MAKE-BELIEVE: A STUDY IN INSTINCT

white body, a black neck, and a bright red knob on its 'nose.' When a flock of them are feeding or resting on the grass, the gauchos approach them quietly on horseback, taking care not to get on the windward side of them, and then suddenly wheel towards them and gallop at full speed, shouting at the top of their voices. The birds are so terrified that they cannot move, and fall easy victims. The gaucho boys also catch another bird, the Silver-bill (*Lichenops perspicillata*), by flinging a stick or a stone at it and then rushing in while it sits absolutely motionless, disabled by fear. In these cases it would seem almost possible to catch the birds by the method so often recommended to children by their elders—by putting a pinch of salt on their tail!

There are other birds which appear not to feign death—if we are still to speak of it as feigning—until they are actually caught. It certainly is not always a sham, whatever we may think about it as a rule, for captured birds sometimes die outright, being, in fact, literally frightened to death; while others drop down dead if they are only chased. Amongst the latter, according to Mr. Hudson, is the Spotted Tinamou, which is also ridden down by gaucho boys. The Tinamous are peculiar birds whose home is in South America, where they are often spoken of as 'partridges,' which they at first sight resemble, though their small head, slender neck, and long bill give them a very distinctive appearance. Darwin was struck by their silliness in allowing themselves to be taken, and in truth they have but poor brains and are lacking in intelligence almost as much as in courage. Now it is not to be supposed that such a foolish bird as this could intentionally play a part with much success, yet we learn that when captured, after a few violent struggles to escape, it drops its head, gasps two or three times, and to all appearances dies, but the very moment it is released, the eyes open wide, there is a rattle of wings, and the bird has flown!

We know that many birds, such as those which inhabit the

MAKE-BELIEVE: A STUDY IN INSTINCT

desert where there is no cover in which they can take refuge, and young birds of numerous kinds, endeavour to avoid capture, when they are alarmed, by crouching down close to the ground and keeping perfectly still, their colour harmonising so perfectly with their surroundings that it is extremely difficult to detect them even at close quarters. But this habit is not to be confounded with death-feigning, for the moment such birds perceive that they have been discovered they take to flight or run away with the utmost speed.

Death-feigning is not confined to birds; we find the same thing amongst mammals, and though this is not the place to speak of them at great length, we may mention as examples the opossum, and a South American fox which lies so still when it is overtaken that it may even be lashed with a whip without showing the slightest sign of life. When we consider all these different cases, it is difficult not to believe that the animal is *not* consciously shamming, but is really for the time being quite insensible and does not know what is taking place, though it may recover suddenly and make a desperate effort to escape.

But what are we to think of those other cases of apparent shamming in which the birds seem to be wounded when their nests or young are in danger? Are they intentionally acting, or do they behave so strangely because they *must*, under the influence of an overpowering instinct? Let us see what it would mean if the bird were knowingly and intelligently playing a part. It would indicate that the bird, which might never have seen a wounded comrade, knew exactly how a wound would affect its movements; it would mean that it knew what effect its behaviour would have upon an enemy; it would mean that it was a most accomplished actor. But that is not all, for we should have to suppose that the bird—often of a species by no means remarkable for its intelligence—could reason with itself somewhat after this fashion: "Hello! here comes a dog, and there are all my little ones playing about! He'll catch

MAKE-BELIEVE: A STUDY IN INSTINCT

them, sure as faith! I had better try to attract his attention and get him out of the way while they hide; if I pretend to be wounded he will run after me, and then they will have time to get away. I must be careful, though, that he doesn't *really* catch me; but I must not move too quickly, or else he won't follow!" Would it not be a very clever bird indeed to think of all that in a moment, and then carry out the plan with skill that a first-rate actor might envy?

No, I think we must give up the idea that any bird is capable of such a deep-laid scheme; it would be a little more than the most cunning of them could devise. But in that case, what is the explanation? Probably it is something like this. Once upon a time, as they say in the fairy-tales—and 'once upon a time' is very long ago in the true fairy-tale of science— when birds began to be very fond of their homes and children, they were so much distressed when they saw their beloved possessions in danger that; although they were dreadfully frightened too, they could not fly straight away, but dashed hither and thither, hardly knowing what they were doing. The enemy, attracted by their strange movements, naturally started off in pursuit, and so the eggs or the little ones escaped.

Now in many things the children and grandchildren and great-grandchildren, and so on, through ever so many generations of animals, behave like their parents; we all know how a dog turns round and round before lying down, because its wild ancestors a thousand generations back had the same trick and turned round thus to make a nice snug bed in the long grass. So with our birds: the chicks of the parent bird who behaved so strangely through anxiety for their welfare would probably themselves act in a similar manner when it was their turn to bring up a family, and so *their* chicks would escape and grow up to carry on the trick; while the chicks of those individuals which just flew straight away would be caught and killed and so never grow up at all, or have any little ones of their own.

MAKE-BELIEVE: A STUDY IN INSTINCT

The birds which tumbled about just enough, so that they both escaped themselves and warded off the danger from their chicks, would be the ones to rear successfully the most families and so perpetuate the race, and in that way the instinct would gradually be perfected. Here we have an instance of what, following the teaching of that great naturalist Charles Darwin, we speak of as 'Natural Selection.'

CHAPTER VII

SPORT AND PLAY

The meaning and importance of play—Fighting games—Playful pecking of tame birds—Nursing and nest-building play—Flying games—Swimming games—'Follow-my-leader'—Hide-and-seek of climbing birds—Swinging—Birds and children—Toys and playthings—Mischief and destructiveness—Practical jokes.

IT has been said that animals do not play because they are young, but that they have their youth because they must play; and it is hardly too much to say that their success in life depends to a great extent on their success in play at this time, for their actions in play are nearly always of a kind not very different from the actions they will have to perform in real earnest later on. In play the animal either is not serious in what it does, or it tries to do things which there is no necessity for it to do at the time, but which, sooner or later, it will have to know how to do unless it is to fare very badly in life. Play forms a most important part of a young animal's education and of an older animal's business training, and if I were asked to say in as few words as possible exactly what animal play is, I think I should describe it as the exercise of instinctive activities just for fun.

The desire to play is itself an instinct, and as it is found in nearly all the higher animals we may be sure that it is a valuable one. It is worth while to consider rather more fully in what way it is so important. Play enables an animal to practise the exercises and actions which are necessary for its existence; in play it gains control and mastery over its body; it learns to move about skilfully—to fly, walk, leap, hop, run, or swim; it

SPORT AND PLAY

becomes agile in hunting its prey, deft in seizing it, strong in holding it; it learns the knack of shaking and disabling it; it learns to lie in wait, to hide, to dodge when running or flying; and it learns to fight and to defend itself. Many of the things it is able to do when grown up, but which it does not know how to do instinctively, it first learns in play.

We must not forget, however, that there are other ways in which animals learn to do things, and one of them is by imitation. All the higher animals have a tendency to imitate the actions of their fellows, and in that way they learn to do a great many things which are themselves by no means playful; but having learnt them by imitation, they often practise them afterwards in play. Young animals, like children, take pleasure in pretending; like children, too, they are full of curiosity, and a desire to 'find out all about it.' They enjoy energetic action; they enjoy making things move; they enjoy doing things which they 'don't have to,' just for the pleasure of doing them.

Fighting games are the favourite form of play amongst many young animals; it is hardly necessary to mention puppies as an example. In the same way, young birds often indulge in mock battles which sometimes become very realistic, especially as the birds grow older. Young Sparrows peck one another vigorously when they have nothing whatever to quarrel about, so far as we can see, and this habit never leaves them. We regard Sparrows as quarrelsome birds, and so they are, but there is little doubt that many of their 'shindies' are without serious foundation or intent. A Sparrow in high spirits chirps aggressively, another Sparrow answers back; then there is a flutter of wings, and all the Sparrows in the neighbourhood hurry to the spot and join in, just for the fun of the thing. A general free fight ensues, with much abusive language and mutual buffeting, but as none of the combatants has any particular grievance against any other the squabble lasts only a few seconds, and then, having given vent to their superabundant

SPORT AND PLAY

high spirits and energy, the birds disperse as suddenly as a little crowd of street urchins at the cry of "Policeman!"

Other Finches also know the fascination of a friendly encounter, but few of them are quite so ready to improvise riotous assemblies as the hooligan Sparrows. Starlings are almost equally quarrelsome, and Wagtails bite and chase one another as enthusiastically as puppies. Young Game-birds thoroughly enjoy a 'scrap,' and it is by no means an uncommon thing to see two youthful Partridges with their wings spread and heads down indulging in a scrimmage.

A favourite amusement of many tame birds is to bite playfully at their master's fingers. If you have ever been on friendly terms with a pet Canary, you are probably familiar with this form of play. A brother of Brehm, the naturalist, had a tame Vulture which used to amuse itself by nibbling his fingers without hurting them, just as a friendly terrier will pretend to bite his owner's hand in play. The mock anger of a tame Bullfinch is very realistic; the bird gapes, hisses, flutters his wings, and ruffles his feathers at his master exactly as he does before a combat with a rival, although the two are on the most friendly terms. A pretence of challenge and combat is the most usual form of animal play, and it is easy to realise how useful it is as a training for real warfare.

But though among wild creatures skill in self-defence, and in attack too, is often a matter of necessity, life is not *all* fighting. There are other, more peaceful, arts which are in their way just as important, and these often have their counterpart in play. Many young birds make themselves useful in the nursery and help to look after their little brothers and sisters. When Canaries have two broods in the season, the youngsters of the first family often feed the nestlings of the second brood. In the same way a family of young Swallows which had themselves not long outgrown the nest have been known to help their parents to feed their little brothers and sisters. Some young birds are even more enterprising, for Altum saw several young Killdees

SPORT AND PLAY

still in their first suit of feathers busy mothering a young Cuckoo.

Young Moorhens have another interesting habit. In many cases the parents have several broods in the same season, the hen beginning to lay again when the first hatch is about a fortnight old. The young of the first brood have therefore to turn out of the nest, but the cock-bird builds another nest for them to rest and sleep in, and immediately on the appearance of the second hatch they assist the old birds in feeding and brooding over them, and then in taking them out in little parties. But this nursery-play goes still further, for they make additional nests for them, like their own, beside the water. Another water-bird, the Dabchick, also indulges in nest-building play, but not quite of the same kind. The Dabchick's nest is a heap of floating weeds and rushes, and as time goes by it becomes more and more sodden and sinks deeper in the water, so that it would disappear altogether beneath the surface if more weeds were not heaped on the top of it. But like many other water-birds, Dabchicks constantly add fresh material to their nest, and as soon as the young are old enough to help in this they do so.

Even old birds sometimes indulge in playful building—'fancy-work' to pass away the time. Whether the 'cock-nests' which are made by certain birds, such as Wrens, are constructed merely in play, or whether they all serve some useful purpose, we do not know. Weaver-birds (*Ploceus*) in captivity spend a great deal of time in the exercise of their craft, and if for any reason they cannot make their peculiar purse-like nests, they still weave, using every available bit of thread or straw to entwine in the bars of their cage, passing it in and out between the wires, knotting it, and weaving such an intricate tangle that it can only be removed by cutting. This is, perhaps, nothing more than the industry of enforced idleness, and it may be that in their wild state the birds are too busy with their serious building and all the family cares that follow to do any weaving for mere amusement.

SPORT AND PLAY

There are a few instances of birds, which were not in the condition commonly known as 'broody,' sitting on eggs that did not belong to them, apparently for nothing but their own amusement. When Mr. Bartlett was in tropical South America he saw a Curassow (*Nothocrax urumutum*) running about amongst the common Fowls in a Peruvian's house. Curassows are fine, handsome birds nearly as large as a Turkey; their home is in the forest, but they are often captured by the natives and kept as pets, becoming quite tame and even affectionate towards their owners.

The particular bird described by Mr. Bartlett was the tyrant of all the domestic animals about the house, and would bully the dogs themselves and drive them out of doors. What was especially interesting was that when one of the Hens began sitting, it drove her off the nest and took her place; but it soon wearied of the game, and one day it destroyed all the eggs, like a bad child who breaks his toys when he is tired of them. As we shall see in another chapter when speaking of Ravens and Magpies, other birds besides Mr. Bartlett's Curassow display a taste for mischievous amusements.

Many species of birds fly for pleasure and perform all kinds of strange antics while on the wing. The Parson-birds of New Zealand, so called on account of two white tufts hanging under their chin like the white bands which used to be worn by clergymen, mount high in the air on fine days in parties of six or more and amuse themselves in a sportive flight accompanied by quite a variety of clever tricks. Moving round in wide circles, they turn and twist, throw somersaults, and parachute down with wings and tail spread wide. Then they dash upwards again and, closing their wings, support themselves in the air for a few moments by rapid beats of the expanded tail; but they cannot maintain their position long in this manner, and soon they begin another parachute descent, with the wings closed. As they come near the ground, the wings are half opened, and they shoot forwards and away, and so on, until at

SPORT AND PLAY

last, as if on some preconcerted signal, they all suddenly dive towards the forest and disappear from sight.

Many different species of birds enl en their flight by turning somersaults, but the only kind with which most people are familiar is the Tumbler Pigeon. Like all other domestic Pigeons the Tumblers are descended from the Rock Dove, which does not tumble, and some people maintain that their performance is therefore not natural. But as Darwin pointed out, the birds could not have been *taught* to perform this trick, and the instinct must have appeared naturally in the first place, though it has been strengthened by the selection of the most skilful birds, probably for hundreds of years. The result is that in the present race of Tumblers there are some wonderful performers. Their usual method is to fly in a close flock to a great height, turning back-somersaults as they rise.

Some birds cannot rise a yard from the ground without turning over, and some spring only a few inches from the floor, turn a neat back-somersault, and alight on their feet. In India there has been for 250 years past a breed which tumble over and over on the ground after being shaken slightly, and do not stop until they either fall exhausted or are taken up and blown upon! This can hardly be regarded as play, for the birds seem to be quite unable to help themselves; they *must* tumble, whether they will or not. But the more ordinary Tumblers appear to have a certain amount of control over their performance, and to enjoy it. A bird that had strayed five miles from the cote and was driven home with stones did not tumble once all the way, but as soon as she came in sight of the cote she darted inside for her mate and the pair together celebrated her return by a grand round of tumbling. Some birds, of the kind known as 'Rollers,' roll over and over so rapidly as they fall through the air for twenty feet or so, that it is impossible to count their turns, and they look like a ball coming down.

Besides antics such as these, and the spirited sporting flight

SPORT AND PLAY

of the Parson-bird, the games indulged in by Cuckoos may appear rather tame, but they are more of the nature of what we usually understand by play. 'Late in the afternoon in May, where these birds are plentiful they resort to some familiar glade or patch of ground dotted over with bushes and join in a sort of 'general post' or 'follow-my-leader,' in which any bird among them is the leader of the moment and is pursued by a companion as she flies from bush to bush to join another bird. The next minute she in her turn may fly away, flitting gracefully across the open ground pursued by a comrade, and so on, restlessly, untiringly, with no apparent plan or order or intention beyond a wish to play or dally with one another in the spring sunshine. The game proceeds noisily with many cries of "*cuckoo!*" and half a dozen breathless variations of the call, sometimes not going beyond a single syllable, a soft "*kūk*," a sharp "*kŭk*," sometimes broken up, as it were, into three, or repeated in various ways.

Snow-Buntings have a boisterous little game of their own, in which a whole flock join. When they are all on the wing, those in advance alight on the ground; the birds coming on behind pass close over and settle in front of them, and so on, until the last birds of the flock are just about to alight, when the first members of the party—which now form the rear ranks, all the others having flown over their heads—take wing again and fly over to the front, and the manœuvre is repeated by numbers of the birds in turn, so that the whole flock appears to be rolling along the ground. The game is played to an unceasing accompaniment of clear call-notes. On meeting with any obstacle or arriving at a place such as the edge of a cliff, which breaks up their party, they all fly off together to a distant spot and begin again.

In his account of the animals which he met with in the desolate Antarctic region, Dr. Wilson gives an amusing description of the playfulness of the Adélie Penguin. The quaint little bird darts about hither and thither in the icy waters like

SPORT AND PLAY

a fish, dashing to and fro beneath the ice floes, bobbing up from the water a hundred yards away with the suddenness of a Jack-in-the-box and leaping on to the ice in sheer play, apparently with no more serious purpose than to wag his tail and squawk a greeting to a comrade far away on the floe. Having accomplished his object, in he dives again and, guiding his course in some wonderful manner, comes up just where he wished.

In the open sea, the birds play a sort of game of follow-my-leader, shooting through the water, propelled by their queer little wings, as fast as fish, gambolling like dolphins, and popping up on the ice floe like rabbits. "Smart, comical, confiding little beasts, the most excellent company imaginable in such a desolate region as the Antarctic, they are like anything in the world but birds." Penguins have two very terrible enemies which pursue them under the water—the Killer Whale and, a little further north amongst the pack-ice, the fierce Sea-Leopard, a huge seal twelve feet in length. Against such creatures as these they are of course quite powerless to defend themselves, and their only means of safety, if one of these animals comes on the scene while they are fishing, is to seek refuge on the ice. There can be little doubt therefore that their follow-my-leader and Jack-in-the-box games serve a useful purpose as a training in agility, on which their life depends, both in obtaining their food and in escaping from their foes.

When climbing birds are alarmed they try to avoid detection by hiding behind a branch or tree-trunk, and they are nearly all very skilful dodgers. It is very difficult indeed to get a glimpse of a Woodpecker if he wants to keep out of sight; he runs round and round the trunk, clings to the bark with his sharp claws, and on whichever side you may be, he always contrives to be on the other. You will therefore not be surprised to learn that the Woodpecker's favourite game is hide-and-seek. These birds are much addicted to play, and

SPORT AND PLAY

often a whole family join in the game, dodging one another round the tree, lying close against the bark with half-opened wings until discovered, darting away, chasing one another, and behaving generally in the most lively and frivolous manner for five minutes at a time.

Other birds are very fond of swinging. We know that this is so in the case of cage-birds such as Parrots and Canaries, which take evident pleasure in swinging on a ring; in a state of nature, Tits and many of the Finches are often seen clinging to the end of a slender bough and swinging on it. I believe Rooks and Crows thoroughly enjoy, on a windy day, being swayed about on the topmost branches of tall trees—at all events if they do not they might easily find a more stable perch lower down. Mr. Hudson and Dr. Sclater describe how White-tailed Kites (*Elanus leucurus*) in the Argentine sport in the high winds. They are handsome birds with ruby-red eyes which contrast finely with the snow-white feathers of their plumage. Their flight is as buoyant as a gull's, and their wing-power is marvellous; like the Martin, they delight to soar in a gale of wind, rising and falling alternately, and will spend hours at a time in this sport. Now and then they seem entirely to abandon themselves to the fury of the gale and are whirled away like thistle-down until, suddenly asserting their power again, they shoot back in the teeth of the wind to their original position. For their most interesting game, however, they require a cluster of tall poplar trees, and the way it is played is as follows. Each bird chooses a separate tree and perches on the slender twigs at the very top, balancing itself there with outspread wings. Then, when the next strong gust comes, they let go; the tree tops, swaying about with the force of the gale, are swept from under them, and the birds remain poised almost motionless in the air until the twigs swing back again to their feet.

Crows and Jackdaws also have a boisterous little game of their own which is played with much zest on a windy day. It

SPORT AND PLAY

consists in one bird suddenly hustling another off the tree or tower where he is perched, and taking his place—just as boys when bathing often push each other from the river-bank into the water.

There is not only a great deal of similarity between the play of many animals and that of children, but in some cases a feeling of fellowship and cordial understanding is shown by the way in which animals and children join in each other's games. This is, of course, most often seen in the case of dogs, but occasionally tame birds have been known to show the same kind of playful friendship. Naumann speaks of a tame Stork whose favourite amusement was to join with children in a game of catch. It used to run after them in the street with outstretched wings and seize their jackets with its bill, and then run away again, looking round to see whether it was being followed. It would in turn allow itself to be caught by the wing, and then once more run after the children. Similarly Günzel relates how a tame Magpie at a school used to go out with the children at playtime and invite them to play by hopping about excitedly and snapping her bill. She preferred the boys, who loved to tease her and tried to catch hold of her tail, but she was too quick for them, for she hopped nimbly aside and dodged so skilfully that it was impossible to touch her, though at other times, when not playing this game, she was quite docile. That it really was a game, and one which she thoroughly enjoyed, was quite evident from the way in which she followed any boy who would play with her, and never seemed to tire of the sport.

Whether Magpies, Jackdaws, Ravens, and other birds look upon the glittering objects of all sorts, which they are so fond of collecting and hiding away, as playthings, it is difficult to say. One frosty morning at the 'Zoo,' Mr. Cornish found the Ravens busy hiding all the pieces of broken ice they could find, in holes round the edges of their aviary. In order to conceal a large fragment more effectually one of the birds pulled it from

WHITE STORK AND HIS PLAYMATES

The Stork's favourite amusement was to join with children in a game of catch, running after them in the street and seizing their jackets with its bill, and allowing itself in turn to be caught by the wing (*page* 120).

White Storks are great favourites in Holland and Germany, where they often nest on roofs and chimneys.

SPORT AND PLAY

the cranny into which it had been poked and carefully rubbed it in sand till it was well covered with a coat of grit before pushing it back again. The same morning "the Gulls were particularly noisy, and playing at a new game with bits of ice, which they picked up from the broken edges of their ponds and let fall on the sound ice. They then scrambled and fought for the pieces as they slid on the slippery surface." One big Gull swallowed his new toy, "a large triangular piece, which stuck for some time in its throat, and evidently gave it much discomfort until the sharp edges melted."

Some birds undoubtedly do have playthings with which they amuse themselves for hours at a time. A Crane will often play ball with a pebble or a bit of earth, tossing it into the air and catching it, or trying to do so, as it falls. I have seen a tame Raven amusing himself with a piece of wood exactly as a dog does, carrying it about, laying it down as an invitation to his master to try to take it away from him, and just at the critical moment picking it up again and dodging.

Girtanner speaks of a Vulture which used to tug at its master's watch-chain and clothing, or pull straws from his hand, "chuckling with delight" meanwhile. Straw appears to have been this bird's favourite plaything and when it saw its master getting ready to plait a straw rope it always joined him at once and stood by until the rope was ready for it to bite and pick to pieces. The padding of its cage was stuffed with straw—a perfect treasure-house of playthings; when the bird discovered this it tore open the cover and proceeded to apply the contents to its own particular use.

Mischief and destructiveness are often near akin to play in birds as in boys. Rey, speaking of his Carolina Parrots, says that their favourite amusement was throwing their water-vessels out of the cage when they had finished drinking, and if the cups broke they gave evident signs of enjoyment.

Linden kept some Cockatoos which *would* turn over the food-trough in their cage. He fastened it to the bars with

SPORT AND PLAY

wire, he screwed it down, and tried all sorts of means to secure it, but the birds knew perfectly well how to unscrew it, and were never satisfied until they had got it loose again; sooner or later they always succeeded in their efforts.

Perhaps Cockatoos are without exception the most destructive of birds, for they will gnaw through planks two inches thick, and even through a thin sheet of iron. Some enterprising birds amongst them are such determined prison-breakers that they will do their best to penetrate a brick wall.

No doubt Dickens exaggerated a little, as was his way, in his story of a Raven that died young, but as in his other exaggerations, the foundation of what he says is true enough. He writes: "It may have been that he was too bright a genius to live long, or it may have been that he took some pernicious substance into his bill, and thence into his maw,—which is not improbable, seeing that he new-pointed the greater part of the garden-wall by digging out the mortar, broke countless squares of glass by scraping away the putty all round the frames, and tore up and swallowed, in splinters, the greater part of a wooden staircase of six steps and a landing."

The variety of Raven (*Corvus corax principalis*) which inhabits the most northerly part of the American continent is credited with being a particularly mischievous bird, and is said to take special pleasure in annoying and teasing dogs. A sleeping dog gives him a fine opportunity for a practical joke, and he delights to arouse the sleeper by dropping a stick or a stone upon him. Only the most highly developed animals and birds, such as Monkeys, Parrots, and Crows, are clever enough to invent jokes of this kind. The various members of the Crow family in America appear to be exceptionally resourceful in such tricks. The American Magpie sometimes imitates the cry of a Hawk and sends poultry running helter-skelter in every direction; on another occasion it will produce a sound so exactly like the cackle of a Hen after she has laid an egg that the rooster is completely deceived by it and hurries to the spot

SPORT AND PLAY

where his lady appears to be, in order to pay her a few courteous attentions, only to discover that it is *vox et præterea nihil*—she is nowhere to be seen. The Blue Jay (*Cyanocitta cristata*) is an even more gifted mimic, for he can imitate to perfection the call-notes, alarm-notes, and cries of distress of quite a number of birds and animals, and delights in doing it for his amusement. Owls he is especially fond of fooling, and sometimes he has the temerity to tease Hawks, which he may do in safety while he keeps to the cover of the woods, but in the open the Hawk sometimes gets his revenge, and the consequences for the Jay are serious.

According to Brehm, the gentle and respectable Ibis (one species of which was regarded as a sacred bird by the Egyptians and figures in their kingly cartouches), is not above occasional practical joking. He writes: "Those I have known lived fairly peacefully with all the other birds sharing their quarters, but domineered to some extent over the weaker ones and took apparent pleasure in teasing them. The Flamingoes were their especial butts, and they had a very curious method of teasing them. While they were asleep, the head buried amongst the feathers, an Ibis would quietly sneak up and peck at their webbed feet, from pure mischief, and not meaning to hurt them." The Flamingo, startled out of his nap by the tickling of his feet, would glance at his tormentor and move away to another spot, but he was not allowed to sleep in peace, for the Ibis was soon after him and indulging in the same pranks.

Numerous other examples of birds' mischievousness, destructiveness, and practical joking might be given, but though they are amusing, such tricks are not play in the true sense of the word, and we must pass them by in order to describe habits which are in many ways more interesting.

CHAPTER VIII

PLAYGROUNDS AND PAVILIONS

The Paradise-bird's playing-tree—Beauty on a pedestal—The Argus Pheasant's drawing-room—A wonderful courtship display—Sexual selection—The Polyplectron's playground and courtship—The club-grounds of Game-birds—Bower-birds and their pleasure-houses—Satin Bower-birds at the 'Zoo'—Decorating the bower—A depôt for lost property—Courtship-play—The Spotted Bower-bird's avenue and playthings—The Regent Bower-bird's love of colour—Carpeted playgrounds—The Gardener-birds and their beautiful pleasure-grounds—The Golden Bower-bird's toy village and triumphal arch.

TO speak of "Birds at Play" seems quite natural and reasonable, for play is what we should expect of creatures nearly all of which are so active and vivacious, and in many cases so intelligent. But when we come to talk of playgrounds and playhouses or pavilions it is quite another matter, for though it is well known that birds have their favourite localities and often remain in the same neighbourhood, and even within a very small area, for considerable periods of time, especially in the nesting season, we are apt to look upon them as wanderers who can, and do, range far and wide, flying where they will, with the world for their parish, and therefore not at all likely to claim one tiny spot upon the ground for their sporting like the less favoured beings who are bound to earth for want of wings. Nor do we expect to find them engaging in architectural pursuits other than the building of nests. Yet birds' playgrounds and playhouses do exist, and though they are by no means common they are not so rare as might be supposed, for a considerable number of species construct them.

PLAYGROUNDS AND PAVILIONS

Short of an actual play-*ground*, the nearest approach to it is a favourite tree which the birds frequent for their social gatherings, and where they amuse themselves with strange antics. The Great Bird-of-Paradise (*Paradisea apoda*), for example, chooses a tall forest tree with an immense head of spreading branches and thin foliage which gives plenty of clear space for play. There a dozen or twenty full-plumaged male birds assemble in the early morning and display their beautiful plumes, raising their wings high over their backs, stretching out their necks, and keeping their rich golden side-feathers in continual vibration. They fly about from branch to branch in great excitement, so that the tree presents a kaleidoscopic scene of dancing colour; and so intent are the birds on play that they can be shot down one after another with arrows by a hunter concealed in a little shelter of palm leaves among the branches.

Many other birds of beautiful decoration have special playing-grounds, where they spend much of their time in attitudinising and displaying their charms. The most fantastically ornamental of them all are the Lyre-birds (*Menuræ*) of Australia. In some respects, as in colour and in the large size of its feet, a Lyre-bird is not much unlike a Megapode, but its wonderful tail is perhaps the most remarkable and peculiar decoration possessed by any bird. The two large, broad, strangely curved outer feathers, whose resemblance to the form of a lyre has given the bird its name, appear at first sight to be notched at intervals, almost from end to end, across the whole width of the inner web, but the seeming notches are really transparent patches of feather of an open texture. In addition to these remarkable feathers they have a number of light filamentous plumes like those of the Paradise-birds. It takes four years for the bird to put on his full livery, and then, alas! he does not retain it long, for the beautiful tail is soon moulted. But while he has it, he is naturally very proud of such a fine possession, and takes great care of it. Going

PLAYGROUNDS AND PAVILIONS

through the brushwood of his native forests he carries it straight out in a line with the body so that it escapes being damaged by contact with the branches; but when he arrives at his playground he raises it on high and spreads it out to show its full beauty.

The playground is a small, round hillock, trampled smooth by the bird's powerful limbs, which are so muscular that he can make a standing jump of ten feet to the branch of a tree and then bound by similar leaps from branch to branch. On the top of this hillock he stands, constantly trampling, scratching, and pecking, while he gracefully droops his wings and moves his tail about to an accompaniment of song. Sometimes it is his own proper song, clear and musical, that he sings; at others it is that of any bird he takes it into his head to imitate, for he is one of the cleverest of bird-mimics. Speaking of the species known as Prince Albert's, Mr. Leycester says: "One of these birds had taken up its quarters within two hundred yards of a sawyer's hut, and he had made himself perfect in all the noises of the sawyer's homestead—the crowing of the cocks, the barking and howling of the dogs, and even the painful screeching of the sharpening or filing of the saw."

Another bird of princely splendour which makes a special playing-ground whereon to disport himself and exhibit the grandeur of his attire is the Argus-Pheasant (*Argusianus argus*). Though it has no gorgeous colours, after the Peacock this is perhaps the most splendidly decorated of all the large birds in existence. Like its namesake it is the possessor of 'a hundred eyes,' the whole of the outer web of its enormous secondary wing-feathers being decorated with circular spots, each of them rather larger than a halfpenny, of white and yellow, shading to a deeper rufous tint, and surrounded by a ring of black, the colour being so beautifully arranged and shaded that each spot or 'eye,' when held in a certain position, looks exactly like a ball resting in a cup. This Argus-Pheasant

PLAYGROUNDS AND PAVILIONS

(there are two other species) inhabits the forests of the Malay Peninsula, Siam, southern Tenasserim, and Sumatra. In some parts of Tenasserim it is quite common, and if a gun be discharged in the forest numbers of the birds begin to utter their loud "*how-how*" note, which is audible fully a mile away. This is the male bird's call-note; the female has quite a different cry, which may be represented by "*how-owoo, how-owoo!*" with the last sound much prolonged, and when calling she repeats the sound more and more rapidly until it ends in a series of "*owoos*" all run together.

Except when she has made her nest, the hen-bird has no fixed abode, but wanders at large in the forest. The cock, on the other hand, chooses an open spot where the ground is level, sometimes in a dark and gloomy ravine shut in by dense canebrake and rank undergrowth, at others on a hill-top where the vegetation is less dense, and there establishes what Mr. Davison, who knew more than any other writer about this bird, called a drawing-room. It is a very unpretentious drawing-room, and is made by simply clearing away all weeds and dead leaves from a space measuring about twenty feet from side to side, until nothing remains but the bare earth. Thenceforth all the bird's spare time is devoted to keeping his drawing-room tidy, and if he finds a dead leaf or a twig or any other kind of litter lying there he never fails to remove it at once.

The Malays are very well aware of this habit and turn it to account in their ingenious method of trapping the bird. They take a narrow splinter of bamboo about eighteen inches long and shave it down until it is as thin as paper and as sharp as a razor; then they fasten one end of it to a stout peg or handle. During one of the bird's expeditions in search of food they enter his drawing-room and drive the peg firmly into the ground. When he comes home again and sees an untidy-looking object rather like a giant grass-blade sticking up right in the middle of his drawing-room floor, the very first thing he does is to try to remove it. He takes hold of it with his

PLAYGROUNDS AND PAVILIONS

beak and gives it a pull; the tiresome thing will not break off easily, as a weed should do, however, and after tugging at it for some time and trying to scratch it up, he begins to be annoyed. But he is determined to get rid of it somehow, so he gives it two or three turns round the neck in order to get a better hold, and taking the peg in his bill, springs backwards with all his might. The peg does not move, but the thin, tough bamboo-shaving tightens up, its sharp edges cut deeply into his neck, and he falls down with his head almost severed from his body.

Another way in which the Malays trap these birds is by erecting a sort of miniature football-goal in the middle of the 'drawing-room,' and slinging from it a heavy block of wood by a string which passes over the cross-bar and is fastened to a peg immediately under the block. In this form of trap the peg is driven into the ground quite lightly, so that the bird can pull it up without much difficulty. As soon as he does so the string is released and the log which hangs from the other end of it falls upon him and crushes him.

Without having recourse to such arts as these it would be extremely difficult to capture the beautiful Argus, for though he spends all the time he can in his clearing, and roosts in the nearest tree, he is an extremely shy bird. However stealthily a hunter may approach the spot where an Argus is quietly pacing to and fro in his drawing-room, uttering his peculiar call, when he gets near enough to peer through the dense surrounding foliage he is almost certain to find that the bird has deserted his clearing and dived into the thicket. We cannot therefore be quite sure how he passes all the time which is spent in his playground.

Mr. Davison thought that he probably dances there, but he never succeeded in catching one amusing himself in this way. It is very likely, however, that in answer to his loud calling he receives visits from the hens which, as we have already mentioned, wander about the forest, and that he entertains them by

PLAYGROUNDS AND PAVILIONS

displaying to their admiring gaze his wonderful attire, just as he has been observed to do in captivity.

He begins by strutting to and fro in front of the hen in order to attract her attention, casting sidelong glances upon her and occasionally shaking his wings in a lively manner, so as to make her understand that he is in a playful mood and quite ready to entertain her if she will but take notice of what he is doing. Having sufficiently aroused her curiosity and prepared her for what is to follow, he halts close in front of her and—*trrrrrh!* with a rattle of quills and rustling of feathers he is suddenly transformed before her very eyes into a great circular screen with one edge on the ground, and in an almost upright position, like a picture on an easel. It may be compared to the sudden opening of a Japanese sunshade. Not a vestige of *bird* remains, for his body and limbs are completely hidden, and even his head is tucked away at the back of the outspread wings so that nothing shall obstruct the hen's view of the wonderful picture he has displayed for her admiration.

The open wings are overtopped by the enormously long tail-feathers, towering high above all the rest, and the shading of the eyes on each great wing-feather is so disposed that, with the light shining from above, every one of them looks exactly like a real ball lying in a real cup. At the same time the smaller wing-feathers, the *primaries*, are turned down in front of the breast near the ground like two little fans or shields, and as every one of these feathers appears to have a second smaller feather of chestnut dotted over with tiny white points painted upon it, the display is very wonderful indeed, and if the hen-bird does not admire all these exquisite patterns she must be very difficult to please. But since even his head is behind the screen, how is the possessor of so much finery to know whether she is pleased or not? By moving his head a little lower he would be able to peep under the edge of the wing and so watch the effect of his display. Some naturalists think that is what he does; but Mr. Bartlett saw the Argus at the 'Zoo' adopt another plan. He noticed that some of the secondary feathers were often rather frayed and worn near the base, and he was at a loss to account for this until he observed one of the birds, while showing off, suddenly pop his head *through* the screen, between two feathers, as though to inquire what he and the hen and the world in general thought of *that* for a show!

Some people declare that amongst birds the female really cares very little about the fine clothes of her wooers and is quite incapable of appreciating their beauty, being far more impressed by a bold and quarrelsome demeanour than by richness of attire. If that were so in all cases such a bird as the Argus would be in sorry plight, for his wonderful decoration and extraordinary attitudes during courtship would be purposeless and entirely wasted, and he seems to be wholly devoid of the fighting spirit. He will even allow himself to be flaunted in his own drawing-room and driven out of the clearing by a Pheasant of another species, rather than attempt to defend his domain, as the following incident, related by Mr. Davison, shows:—

"I had stalked an Argus, and while waiting to obtain a good shot, I heard the peculiar note, a sort of '*chukun, chukun*' followed by the whirring noise made by the male Fireback,[1] and immediately after saw a fine male Fireback run into the open space, and begin to chase the Argus round and round its clearing. The Argus seemed loth to quit its own domain, and yet not willing to fight, but at last being hard pressed it ran into the jungle. The Fireback did not attempt to follow, but took up a position in the middle of the clearing and recommenced the whirring noise with his wings, evidently as a challenge, whereupon the Argus slowly returned, but the moment it got within the cleared space, the Fireback charged it, and drove it back into the jungle, and then, as before, took up his position in the middle of the space and repeated the challenge. The Argus immediately returned, but only to be again driven back, and this continued at least a dozen times, and how much longer

[1] The Fireback Pheasant of Tenasserim (*Lophura rufa*).

PLAYGROUNDS AND PAVILIONS

it would have continued I cannot say, but a movement on my part attracting the birds' attention, they caught sight of me, and instantly, before I could fire, disappeared into the jungle. The Argus never made the slightest attempt to attack the Fireback, but retreated at once on the slightest movement of the latter towards it, nor did I see the Fireback strike the Argus with either bill, wings, or spurs."

I do not know whether the Polyplectron, a near relative of the Argus, is equally peaceable in its disposition, but this is hardly likely because the cock-bird has weapons on his legs, in the form of double spurs, which mark him out for a fighter, and look quite capable of making short work of an adversary. The Polyplectron is a splendid little Pheasant which inhabits almost the same region of the world as the Argus, but is rather scarce and local. In the island of Palawan, to the north of Borneo, Mr. Whitehead found it in only one forest. Like the Argus, it makes a clearing in some unfrequented spot and keeps it neatly swept. Right in the middle of the ring, which is much smaller than the Argus's drawing-room, there is often a hump of earth, where the bird no doubt stands, as on a pedestal, to show off his fine feathers; for though he is a much smaller bird than the Argus, he is hardly less wonderfully adorned, and is even more ingenious than that bird in striking attitudes when courting. His feathers are marked with brilliant eyes like those on a Peacock's train, but in his case the ornaments appear on the wings as well.

Now when a Peacock wants to be seen to the best advantage by his lady-love, he stands facing her, because he has to show her his beautiful blue throat and breast as well as his wonderful tail. But there is nothing very attractive about the Polyplectron's breast, which is rather dull and sombre than otherwise; so he turns it away, out of sight, while he raises and spreads his tail and twists it a little to one side, at the same time dropping the nearer wing and raising the opposite one. In this ingenious attitude he struts before the admiring female

PLAYGROUNDS AND PAVILIONS

with every 'eye' he possesses turned towards her. If she walks over to the other side of him, he at once changes front, throwing up the opposite wing and giving his tail a twist so that she may still see only what is most beautiful in his plumage.

Both the Argus and the Polyplectron, then, make little private playgrounds where they spend their time either in solitude or with only one spectator to admire their antics; but many Game-birds have a sort of club-ground where they meet and sport in company, and that is, of course, in some ways far more interesting. Being Game-birds, however, they seem to be unable to play without quarrelling, and as there is a great deal to be told about their doings I think we had better reserve them until we come to consider the courtship of birds, when we shall have to speak about their dancing parties and tournaments.

We now come to one of the most remarkable circumstances in bird-life. In the Australian region, the home of the Mound-Builders (whose curious 'incubators' we have already described), and of the strangely adorned and interesting Lyre-birds, there dwells a family known as the *Ptilonorhynchidæ* or Bower-birds. There is nothing very extraordinary in the appearance of these birds, which are about the size of a Jackdaw (to which they are allied) and usually by no means bright in colour, though some of them have gaily coloured crests or particularly glossy plumage. Their claim to distinction lies in their astonishing habit of building arbours and playhouses, or pavilions, which are in some cases surrounded by elaborate pleasure-grounds, and are the most curious of the many strange examples of bird architecture. These arbours or bowers have nothing to do with the nests which the birds build, and which are of quite an ordinary kind, being not unlike that of our own Jay. On the contrary, they are designed and erected and laid out for amusement and play, and for nothing else. Every kind of Bower-bird has its own peculiar style of architecture; some of the bowers are quite simple in form and others are more

PLAYGROUNDS AND PAVILIONS

elaborate, but they are all so strange that if you came across one and did not know that it had been made by a bird, I think you would be quite sure that you had at last discovered the real home of a fairy.

The species of Bower-bird which is best known in this country is the Satin Bower-bird (*Ptilonorhynchus violaceus*), whose name is derived from his beautiful glossy blue-black plumage, which shines like satin in the sunlight. He has, besides, large and lustrous eyes of azure blue, set in a circle of coral red, and is altogether a handsome bird in spite of his quiet colouring. The female is greenish in colour and by no means so glossy as her husband, though she of course shares his name. Both male and female may be seen in our Zoological Gardens, where you may often find them at play and watch the cock-bird building his bower.

The bower is built of slender twigs, arranged in the form of a very short avenue, open, of course, at both ends. Some of the twigs are curved and cross each other overhead, so that on looking through the bower you see that the top of the tunnel is pointed, like a Gothic arch. Only a few of the twigs meet in this way, however, so the roof is not really closed in, but is formed of a delicate open network or tracery. The ends of the twigs of which the sides of the bower are built are firmly interwoven into a platform of sticks which forms the floor. The male bird is the chief worker, though his partner sometimes helps him a little in his task.

When the building is finished, or perhaps even sooner, the birds turn their attention to the decoration, and in this they show a curious fancy. In the Gardens they use any bright-coloured objects which are supplied by their keeper, such as bits of wool, shreds of cloth, or scraps of paper, but in their native forests, where the bowers are found in remote spots under the shelter of overhanging branches, they collect gaudy Parrots' feathers and dead leaves for the adornment of their playing-ground. What they particularly fancy, however, are

PLAYGROUNDS AND PAVILIONS

shells and the bleached bones of animals, which are sometimes found in great numbers at the entrance to the bower. In one bower, which was photographed by Mr. North, there were twelve pieces of wallabies' bones, three pieces of moss, a spray of acacia blossom, some eucalyptus cones, seven shells, and the egg-bag of a spider—as miscellaneous a collection of playthings as one would find in a small boy's pocket. The fact is, these Bower-birds are such inveterate collectors that they will appropriate almost any object of a suitable size that they come across, and this habit is so well known to the natives that when any small ornament or similar object is missing they make a point of going round first of all to all the bowers in the neighbourhood to look for it. Mr. Gould once found a stone tomahawk amongst the birds' treasures, and in another instance the edifice was decked with a variety of blue woollen scraps which had no doubt been stolen from some neighbouring settlement.

These objects are used as playthings as well as for the decoration of the bower, and even for the adornment of the male bird during courtship. There is very little doubt that all the playgrounds made by birds are in some way connected with courtship, though they are used for amusement as well. That is what we should expect if we are right in believing that animal play of all kinds is really preparation or practice for the more serious business of their lives, for what is more important to a bird than the winning of a mate? We therefore find that there is courtship play just as there is hunting or fighting play, or nest-building play, or flying games.

When the Bower-bird is wooing his lady he behaves in a very energetic manner. He chases her about, seizes a gay feather or a large leaf in his bill (no doubt to make himself more beautiful, just as a human wooer is sometimes known to put a flower in his buttonhole), utters a curious kind of note, ruffles his feathers, runs round the bower, and becomes so excited that his bright eyes seem almost to start out of his head. He opens

PLAYGROUNDS AND PAVILIONS

first one wing and then the other, whistles, pretends to pick up something from the ground, and exercises every art which could possibly prove attractive to the lady of the bower, until at last she can no longer resist his allurements.

The Spotted Bower-bird (*Chlamydodera maculata*) is more ambitious in its architecture than the species which we have just described. Its arbour, like that of the Satin-bird, has the form of an avenue, but it is two or three feet long, and is built on a different principle. In the first place, instead of making a platform of sticks to support the walls, these birds, like ourselves, prefer underground foundations, and dig a trench on each side in which they plant the ends of their sticks, so as to form an arched walk. Then they line the walls with tall grasses so disposed that their heads nearly meet, and cleverly kept in their places by stones placed on the ends of the stems along the floor of the avenue. At each end the stones diverge from the entrance, so as to form a little path on either side. The Spotted Bower-birds are even more industrious collectors than the Satin-bird, for they accumulate as much as half a bushel of shells, stones, bones and skulls of small animals, and other objects, at each entrance to the bower. Mr. North discovered a bower in which the birds' originality and inventive genius had led them to construct a second arch over the middle of the first one by continuing the upward curve of the twigs, and the architects had added several Eley's cartridge-cases to their decorations.

The birds visit the deserted camp-fires of the natives in search of bones and other "unconsidered trifles," but the smooth, round pebbles and some of the shells can only be obtained from rivers and streams, or from the sea-shore, and as these are often at a considerable distance from the bowers—in some cases several miles away—a great deal of labour must be spent on the collection. Mr. Lumholtz[1] says: "There are frequently hundreds of shells, about three hundred in one heap

[1] *Among Cannibals.*

PLAYGROUNDS AND PAVILIONS

and fifty in the other. There is also usually a handful of green berries partly inside and partly outside of the bower; but like the empty shells and the other things collected, they are simply for amusement. . . . This bower-bird has another remarkable quality, in its wonderful power of imitating sounds. When it visits the farms, where it commits great depredations in the gardens, it soon learns to mew like a cat or to crow like a cock."

The shells are not regarded by the birds merely as ornaments; they are true playthings, with which they amuse themselves for hours at a time. The Great Bower-bird, for instance, picks up a shell from one heap and, carrying it in its beak, runs through the archway and adds it to the pile at the opposite end. It then chooses another shell from the second heap and hurries back with it, and so on, taking a shell from each side alternately and flitting to and fro through the bower.

The handsome Regent Bower-bird (*Sericulus melinus*), whose bower is very much like that of the Satin-bird, gives evidence of much artistic taste, using berries of several kinds and colours, young shoots of a pinkish tint, and freshly gathered leaves, for the adornment of its playhouse. The ground beside the bower is swept clear of leaves, and here the male bird has been seen jumping about, puffing out his feathers, rolling over, and indulging in all sorts of queer antics. Two other species, *Scenopœus* and *Ailurœdus*, build no bower at all, but prepare an elaborate playground by first making a clearing six or eight feet wide, and then spreading over it a beautiful green carpet of leaves and grasses. Mr. Lumholtz describes how, on one of his excursions amidst the dense scrub on a mountain-top, his attention was attracted by the loud and unceasing voice of a bird. On approaching the spot whence the sound proceeded he found a modest little grey bird, about the size of a thrush, the *Scenopœus dentirostris*. The bird had been neatly arranging a number of large fresh leaves side by

PLAYGROUNDS AND PAVILIONS

side on the black soil, and was singing happily over his work. As soon as the leaves fade they are replaced by new ones, so that the bird always has a nice bright carpet to play on. "On this excursion," Mr. Lumholtz writes, "I saw three such places of amusement, all near one another, and all had fresh leaves from the same kind of trees, while a large heap of dry, withered leaves was lying close by. It seems that the bird scrapes away the mould every time it changes the leaves, so as to have a dark background, against which the green leaves make a better appearance. Can any one doubt that this bird has the sense of beauty?

"The bird was quite common. Later on I frequently found it on the summit of the Coast Mountains in the large scrubs, which it never abandons. The natives call it *gramma*—that is, the thief—because it steals the leaves which it uses to play with."

We have already seen that the taste of the several kinds of Bower-birds differs: one species collects the blue tail-feathers of Parrakeets, bleached bones, and shells; another has a fondness for smooth pebbles and tall grasses; some show a preference for large green leaves, and some for berries. But none show such a lively sense of the beautiful as the Gardener-birds, whose wonderful arbours and pleasure-grounds are perhaps the most marvellous examples of animal art. Mr. Wallace thought that there was no good reason for believing that birds take any delight in colour for its own sake; according to his view, a Bower-bird would only rejoice in bright berries because they are often good to eat. But the Spotted Bower-bird and the Regent-bird collect berries merely to play with, to carry about, and to arrange and rearrange amongst the twigs of the bower; and the case is even stronger in favour of the Gardener-birds, which gather not only berries, but bright orchids and other beautiful flowers, which they use in making for themselves lovely gardens with mossy lawns and the most delightful little summer-houses you could imagine.

PLAYGROUNDS AND PAVILIONS

These fascinating birds live in New Guinea, where bright blossoms and brilliant berries are plentiful. We owe the earliest description of their fairy-like gardens to Dr. Beccari, an Italian naturalist. The species which he met with was the Gardener-bird known as *Amblyornis inornata*, and I think we had better let him tell us in his own words exactly what he saw, leaving out a little here and there because the account is rather long.

He says: "I had just killed a small new species of Marsupial which balanced itself on the stem of a great tree like a Squirrel; and turning round, I suddenly stood before a most remarkable specimen of the industry of an animal. It was a hut or bower close to a small meadow enamelled with flowers, on a diminutive scale. After well observing the whole, I gave strict orders to my hunters not to destroy the little building. That, however, was an unnecessary caution, since the Papuans take great care never to disturb these nests or bowers, even if they are in the way.

"While I was there, neither host nor hostess were at home, and I could not wait for them. My hunters saw them going in and out, when they watched their movements to shoot them. I could not ascertain whether this bower was occupied by one pair, or by several pairs of birds—whether the male alone was the builder, or whether the wife assisted in the construction. I believe, however, that such a bower lasts for several seasons.

"The *Amblyornis* selects a flat, even place around the trunk of a small tree, about as thick and as high as a medium-sized walking-stick. It begins by constructing at the base of the tree a kind of cone, chiefly of moss, of the size of a man's hand. The trunk of the tree becomes the central pillar, and the whole building is supported by it. On the top of the central pillar twigs are then methodically placed in a radiating manner resting on the ground, leaving an aperture for the entrance; thus is obtained a conical and very regular hut. When the work is

PLAYGROUNDS AND PAVILIONS

complete many other branches are placed so as to make the whole quite firm and impermeable to wet. A circular gallery is left between the walls and the central cone, the whole bower being about three feet in diameter. All the stems used by the *Amblyornis* are the thin stems of an orchid forming large tufts on the mossy branches of great trees, easily bent like a straw, and generally about twenty inches long. The stalks had the leaves, which are small and straight, still fresh and living on them, which leads me to the conclusion that this plant was selected by the bird to prevent rotting and mould in the building, since it keeps alive for a long time.

"The refined sense of the bird is not satisfied with building a hut. It is wonderful to find that it has the same ideas as a man; that is to say, that what pleases the one gratifies the other. The passion for flowers and gardens is a sign of good taste and refinement. I discovered, however, that the inhabitants of Mount Arfak did not follow the example of the *Amblyornis*, for their houses were quite inaccessible from dirt.

"Now let me describe the garden of *Amblyornis*. Before the cottage there is a meadow of moss; this is brought to the spot and kept free from grass, stones, or anything which would offend the eye. On this green turf, flowers and fruit of bright colours are placed so as to form a pretty little garden. The greater part of the decoration is collected round the entrance to the arbour; and it would appear that the husband offers there his daily gifts to his wife. The objects are very various, but always of a vivid colour. There were some fruits like a small-sized apple; others were of a deep yellow colour in the interior. I saw also small rosy fruits, and beautiful rosy flowers of a splendid new *Vaccinium*. There were also fungi and mottled insects placed on the turf. As soon as the objects are faded, they are moved to the back of the hut."

The first specimens of the Gardener-bird which were described were all either hens or immature males, which are dull and 'unadorned,' as the Latin name implies. It was not until

PLAYGROUNDS AND PAVILIONS

twenty years afterwards, quite recently, when the adult male was discovered, that he was found to possess an enormous crest of brilliant orange; he is still called by naturalists *inornata*, however, though his baptismal name, like that of many other bipeds, is particularly inappropriate.

On the mountains at the opposite, that is to say the southeast, end of the island of New Guinea, other species of Gardener-birds have since been discovered, and in these also the females are unadorned and the males have beautiful crests. One of these birds is called *Amblyornis musgravianus* because it was found on Mount Musgrave. Like its relatives, it is a lively and keen-sighted bird and very shy, so that a great deal of patience is required to observe it at play. Mr. Goodwin describes its bower as being constructed of moss, in the form of a fountain-basin. The rim is about two feet high from the ground, but the cup is quite shallow, so that the bird can see what is going on in the neighbourhood while he is playing inside it. The mossy lining is beautifully smooth and even, and from the centre, where the jet of water would be in a real fountain, there springs a small tree on which the bird amuses himself by arranging twigs, uttering meanwhile the clear, sharp notes of his song.

During the return journey, while on Mount Belford, Mr. Goodwin tells us that the member of his party from whom that mountain takes its name brought into camp a different kind of Bower-bird, very similar to the Mount Musgrave bird, but smaller. It was a specimen of the Gardener-bird known as *Amblyornis subalaris*, and Mr. Goodwin did not leave the mountain until he had been to look at its playground. "At a short distance off," he tells us, "the bower from the back looks like a cartload of sticks rounded on the top. On going round to the front I saw the most beautiful building ever constructed by a bird, to which, however, my poor description cannot do justice. The edifice was dome-like, only half covered over, and exposed to view inside a ring or circus. In the centre of this

PLAYGROUNDS AND PAVILIONS

was built a bank of moss, decorated with flowers and seed, out of which grew a small tree interlaced with sticks. . . . I was certainly well rewarded for my trouble on this occasion, and felt much indebted to Mr. Belford for having shown me the most interesting sight which I witnessed during the whole of the expedition."

The charming picture which Mr. Vanderlyn has made for us will give you a better idea than any description of what this wonderful playhouse is like. But to realise fully its beauty you must know that the floor is covered with a carpet of the greenest and most delicate moss; you must imagine the brightness of the moss-covered pillar in the centre, gaily decorated with flowers; and, finally, you must picture to yourself the bird's crest of shining gold, and the glittering wing-cases of beetles which he loves to have among his toys; and then I think that you will agree that the life of a bird which can make and possess such beautiful things must be very romantic indeed.

One other Bower-bird we will mention, and then we must take leave of these fascinating creatures. For this, the Golden Bower-bird (*Prionodura newtoniana*), we must return to Australia, where, in Queensland, he makes his home. No Bower-bird is more beautiful, and none more clever. He is clothed from head to tail in golden-coloured feathers, and bears on his head a broad crest of the same bright hue; but his wife is garbed in sober plumage of olive-brown. The Lyre-bird is not a more accomplished mimic. He will croak like a tree-frog; he will utter a low, soft, musical whistle with the most pathetic air; and then he will break into an astonishing variety entertainment in which he gives imitations of all his neighbours. But his skill is not confined to one of the arts, for not even the beautiful gardens and pavilions of the New Guinea Gardener-bird are more remarkable than the elaborate pleasure-grounds which these Queensland birds prepare.

Around two trees, or a tree and a bush, they begin by erecting huge piles of sticks, heaping them up in the form of a cone

PLAYGROUNDS AND PAVILIONS

or pyramid to a man's height. These stick pyramids are four or five feet apart, and one of them is always considerably higher that the other. The birds then fetch from the surrounding scrub long pieces of the thin, flexible stems of creepers, and trail them from one heap of sticks to the other, in such quantities that at last the two pillars are converted into a great archway. The builders next turn their attention to the decorations. In the woods they gather tufts of white moss which they fix all over the pillars and roof of the structure, and last of all, bunches of green berries, like wild grapes, which are hung in clusters from the top. But still they are not satisfied, for all around their great bower they make little huts by bending together the strong stems of standing grass and roofing them over with a flat thatch of slender twigs, until at last the pleasure-ground looks exactly like a miniature model of a native camp with a beautiful triumphal arch in the middle.

Birds of all ages and both sexes resort to this place of amusement. Young and old, male and female, they pursue each other in and out of the grassy huts and through and over the archway, playing merrily to their hearts' content.

CHAPTER IX

COURTSHIP

Excess of bachelors amongst birds, and its results—Arts of peace—Singing for a mate—The meaning of song—Song and dance—Instrumental music —The drumming of Snipes—Courtship flights—The dalliance of Eagles— Antics of Game-birds—The indifference of hens—Bustards in Spain— Coyness and provocation—Feminine boldness: the Northern Phalarope —Good-humoured rivalry: the Flickers.

IF we are sufficiently observant we may find something to interest us in the habits of birds at all times; or at all events in the ways of wild birds, for it must be admitted that birds in captivity often lose a great deal of their spirit and energy because they are deprived of both the necessity and the opportunity of exercising their natural powers. In the case of the more precocious birds, such as the common Fowl, the first days of life after they have escaped from the egg are, I incline to think, usually the most interesting and wonderful of all; but speaking of birds in general there are two periods which particularly attract attention. These are the time of wooing and, a little later, the time when the care of a young family absorbs all the energies of the attentive parents. As a rule it is the female who is seen at her best in bringing up the brood, and the male during courtship, but it must not be supposed that this is so in all cases.

Nature is very wise, and no male bird remains a bachelor if he can avoid it, nor does any female long despise the attentions of a worthy suitor. But so far as we are able to judge, there are more males than females in bird society, with the result that while every hen almost certainly obtains a mate, great numbers of

COURTSHIP

cock-birds fail to do so. Even amongst birds, therefore, the privilege of winning a wife is not to be attained without some individual merit, and often not without strife.

The methods by which the male bird woos her whom he wishes to make his partner are many, and very different amongst the various classes of birds. What we usually find is, that whatever a particular kind of bird excels in at ordinary times, he does especially well when he is courting, and employs as a means of winning the object of his desires. He exercises to the utmost every charm, and tries to exhibit himself in the best light in order to rival his fellows. The older he is, and the more experienced, the more skilful and confident he becomes in his wooing; his energy and determination increase with his skill in practising the arts of his kind, and with them his success as a wooer increases.

As the season of love approaches, the song-bird practises his notes and perfects his song; he sings his loudest and sweetest—or if his voice be not sweet, his harshest and hoarsest—but always, no doubt, according to the taste of the species to which he belongs, his best. It is the song-bird which can most afford to rely on the exercise of his art to gain a mate. Other birds, far more than he, must wander from place to place seeking her, but a song-bird will perch where he can be heard to the best advantage and endeavour to attract her from afar with passionate melody. He expresses all his spirit and strength and longing in song, and when at last the female answers the call, his joy and exultation. In song he invites her to come to him, and dares any other male within hearing to enter into rivalry with him. He is pleading, imperious, persuasive, boastful, triumphant.

True song ought perhaps to be distinguished from the call-notes, danger-signals, cries of alarm or challenge and defiance, and so forth, which are uttered by birds, though it is sometimes difficult to say exactly what is song and what is not. The cry of the Cuckoo, for example, is not song in the narrow sense; but as it is a call-note to attract a mate it is a part of the bird's

COURTSHIP

courtship. It is never uttered except during the pairing season.

Darwin considered that bird-song originated as a method of courtship, and he was probably right, though some naturalists think he was mistaken. They point out that many birds sing long before and long after the mating season, at times when there is no thought of courtship; but that does not prove that the original object of song was not to win a mate, any more than the fact that birds fly when there is no necessity for them to do so, either to seek food or to escape an enemy, proves that those were not the causes in which flight originated.

All the higher animals do things in play which they are not obliged to do at the time, but which are at some time or other necessary for their existence, and they enjoy performing these actions. So many birds practise singing, and take pleasure in it, at times when song is not of any particular immediate use to them. The Redbreast and the Wren are familiar examples of birds that sing all the year round except during hard frost and at the time of moulting. But the consummate master of song, the Nightingale, loses his singing voice as soon as his chicks are hatched; the passionate melody which thrilled us while he was courting his mate and entertaining her at the time of brooding is exchanged for a guttural croak of alarm and anxiety, and if all go well he sings no more until the following spring. If all go well, we say; for it is a remarkable fact that if any accident deprive him of nest or little ones at this early time, he once more recovers his singing voice and so charms his mate that she is content to undertake again the toil of building a new nest and to endure the weariness of brooding once more; and that surely teaches us the true original purpose and meaning of song. There are those who believe that a bird's song is merely an expression of his superfluous vitality and enjoyment of life; but though joyousness, and other emotions too, do find utterance in melody, we must still consider song as being chiefly and preeminently an act of courtship.

COURTSHIP

Sometimes several males will sing in rivalry for the favour of the same female. Skylarks often do so. These birds pair in early spring, when the cold March winds are drying up the broad, open lands where they love to make their nests, and the first flowers are beginning to make the hedgerows bright with colour. Frequently at this time a female may be seen flying swiftly through the air pursued by several males, who toy with her, flutter round her, and burst into snatches of joyous song. Hither and thither they dart, until at last she takes refuge in the herbage and crouches low. Soon she is discovered by one of her suitors, who hovers above her singing sweetly, or alights and runs before her with raised crest, trying in various ways to win her favour. Again she takes wing, and the pursuit is renewed in the same playful, joyous manner. Sometimes a male actively resents the presence of rivals, and they begin to chase each other until, perhaps, the arts of peace give place to active warfare and the strongest and boldest remains in possession of the field.

It has been noticed that some of our songsters, of which the Redbreast is one, at certain moments in their wooing, exchange their loud, clear, rippling song for low, vibrating notes which can scarcely be heard a few yards away. This whispered melody is uttered only when the mate is perched close by, and is usually accompanied by bowing and posturing, or by quick little dancing steps.

Unlike the Skylark, most of our true melodists sit still on their perch while singing; but among foreign birds there are many whose courtship song is accompanied by antics, though it is seldom that the song of such birds is remarkable for its sweetness. Many of the family of American birds which are commonly known as Troupials and Grackles, Starling-like birds with some of the character of our Buntings, indulge in such antics, and especially the Cowpen-birds, whose courtship habits have been described by Mr. Hudson. The male Screaming Cow-bird of La Plata puffs out his plumage like a strutting Turkey-cock and hops briskly up and down his perch in a lively

COURTSHIP

dance, with wings and tail spread out and trailing low, while he utters a hollow-sounding note which ends in a sharp bell-like ring. The female replies with an excited scream, and the dance ends. The common Cow-bird, which has rich violet plumage, puffs out his glossy feathers and rapidly flutters his wings during his song, which begins on a series of deep internal sounds followed by clear, ringing, musical notes. He then suddenly leaves his perch and flutters away over the ground like a huge moth for twenty or thirty yards, when he turns aside and circles round the female, singing loudly all the time and "hedging her in with melody."

Birds which have no singing voice use such vocal powers as they may possess with equal effect in their wooing. The Great Black-backed Gull (*Larus marinus*) fills the air with his harsh, laughing cries when the flocks assemble in the early summer, until the rocks echo again, and no doubt impresses his mate as much by his furious shouting—if we may use the word in speaking of a bird—as by his more or less graceful bowing as he swims around her. Even the male Swan manages to croon a little love-song of a sort. With wings expanded and head held proudly erect, he places himself opposite his mate and utters a curious little double note, the first part of which is very short and glides into the second part, a semitone higher. The female responds with a similar cry half a note lower. Fortunately they do not both sing at the same time!

The birds which do not excel as vocalists, but produce what Darwin referred to as *instrumental* music, practise their art with great vigour at the season of pairing. The Snipe 'drums' his loudest; the Nuthatch makes such a clatter with his bill against a dead bough that he can be heard two or three hundred yards off; the Woodpecker hammers with all his might; and the clapping of the Stork can be heard when the bird himself is so far away as to be invisible. Other birds produce all kinds of strange noises by means of their quill feathers or by beating with their wings.

COURTSHIP

The 'drumming' or 'bleating' of the Snipe was long a puzzle to naturalists and sportsmen, for nobody could explain satisfactorily how the sound was produced. The bird flies to a great height, and after zigzagging about for a little while descends to earth at a terrific speed, with tail outspread and wings a-quiver; and it is then that the strange humming sound is heard. During the descent the two outer tail-feathers are spread out beyond the rest. These feathers are of a peculiar shape, and it has been ascertained that if they be fixed firmly in a cork, attached to a short stick on the end of a string, and whirled round, a typical 'drumming' is produced. There is no doubt that in the living bird it is similarly caused by rapid movement of these feathers through the air during the earthward plunge. While giving this instrumental performance the bird utters calls which sound like *tinker, tinker, tinker,* and is answered by a quick little *djepp, djepp, djepp* in a different key.

The Double or Solitary Snipe (*Scolopax major*), which visits Great Britain in small numbers every autumn, drums while on the ground by throwing back its head almost on to its back and rapidly opening and shutting its beak like a Stork, the result being a noise which resembles that caused by running one's finger along the edge of a comb.

Certain small perching birds of South America called Manakins have some of the secondary wing-feathers in the male of an extraordinary form, with a solid horny lump on the shaft, and give remarkable instrumental performances. One species, *Manacus candœi,* begins with a sharp sound like the crack of a whip, following it up with a harsh rattle like the turn of a key when winding a clock. Rattle and snap and whirr and whizz are variously combined in the courtship of other members of this curious family, till it seems hardly possible that so much noise can be produced by birds so small.

Another South American bird, one of the Guans (*Penelope*), rushes down through the air with outstretched wings, which give

COURTSHIP

forth a crashing sound like the falling of a tree. The Guans are Game-birds; other members of the order produce curious sounds in various ways—by striking their wings together or violently beating the air with them, and so on.

For the present we will leave the musicians, both vocal and instrumental, and consider how the birds which are especially remarkable for their powers of flight conduct their courtship. Foremost amongst these are the Birds-of-Prey, nearly all of which, except Owls and some Falcons, join with their mates in wonderful aerial dances. Eagles, Peregrines, Kestrels, and Buzzards circle round and round each other and ring up to the sky, where they perform marvellous tricks of flight, whirling in their giddy course for hours at a time until, having sufficiently displayed the power of wing which is so important to them in making provision for a hungry family, they glide to a perch and practise other arts. But they are never so majestic as when in flight, and even the mighty Condor looks an awkward creature when, his head bowed and wings spread wide, he hops round his mate with clumsy little steps, making strange murmuring sounds.

The courtship flight of a pair of Eagles has often been described. Brehm, writing of the Bateleur Eagle of Africa, speaks of it as "an incomparable mountebank performance in the air, a bewildering acrobatic display, which seems to unite in itself all the arts of flight practised by all the other Birds-of-Prey." Perhaps we get the finest picture of all in Walt Whitman's description of the dalliance of Eagles "high in space together"—

> The clinching interlocking claws, a living, fierce, gyrating wheel,
> Four beating wings, two beaks, a swirling mass tight grappling,
> In tumbling turning clustering loops, straight downward falling,
> Till o'er the river pois'd, the twain yet one, a moment's lull,
> A motionless still balance in the air, then parting, talons loosing,
> Upward again on slow-firm pinions slanting, their separate diverse flight,
> She hers, he his, pursuing.

COURTSHIP

Reading it, we can almost hear "the sudden muffled sound" and see the mad, tumultuous, downward rush, arrested at the very moment when it seems that both birds must inevitably be plunged together into the river below.

The smaller Birds-of-Prey are hardly less wonderful in their gambols. Watch a pair of Harriers starting on such a flight. It begins tamely enough, the female flying on ahead as though quite unconscious that she is attended, followed by the male, who appears to be only half willing to escort her. But in a moment all that changes. He dashes forward, overtakes her, sweeps round and round, and then deliberately turns his back upon her and soars to the clouds on hurrying pinions. Suddenly, at a great height, he turns right over and with folded wings shoots head downwards, like an arrow, towards his companion. His wings fly open again, and once more he is dashing round and round her, carried on by the tremendous speed of that plunge from the clouds. At last she can resist the invitation no longer; her unresponsive mood is past, and she joins merrily in his gambols.

Other birds less powerful in flight than the Birds-of-Prey, but some of them hardly less skilful, feel the same impulse to use their wings in courtship. The Swallow who has been perched close beside his mate warbling his faint little song suddenly leaves his perch and, followed at once by the female, dashes off with her in a mazy flight, singing as he goes. Or at dusk, when the Nightjar makes his strange, whirring sounds as he crouches lengthwise on a bough, his mate comes to his calling, and together they dance through the air in beautiful curves.

The cries produced by members of the Nightjar family are very curious. In America the best known of these cries is the "*whip-poor-will*" uttered by the bird of that name. Captain Bendire, in his book on North American birds, tells how he witnessed a most amusing performance of a pair of Whippoor-wills whose trysting-place was a heap of sand just beside an outhouse. One evening when he happened to be in the

COURTSHIP

shed soon after sundown his attention was attracted by the familiar Whip-poor-will cry uttered quite close at hand. Peering through a small opening, he saw the bird waddling over the sand-heap in an excited manner, so much interested in its own vocal performance that it did not discover it was being watched. The call was repeated with such rapidity that the sound issued from the bird's great gaping mouth almost in one continuous roll. In a few seconds another bird appeared and joined the first; the new arrival was a female, and she at once lowered her head and answered the impatient calling with a low "*gaw-gaw-gaw*" of endearment. The male sidled up to her and for a moment their bills touched; but then she began to move slowly aside, followed closely by her mate. Presently, however, the movement was reversed—he became coy, and she followed; and so on, from minute to minute, bold and coy by turns, until the house-dog, an inveterate enemy of all Whip-poor-wills, appeared on the scene and put the lovers to flight. On subsequent evenings they did not arrive so early and so were not seen again, though fresh tracks in the sand showed that they continued to make the same spot their place of meeting.

The courtship dances are often wild, ecstatic performances accompanied by strange sounds, and ending in a mad whirl in concert or in a transport of excitement which makes the birds oblivious to what is taking place around them.

The Game-birds are the most famous of bird-dancers, and nearly all of them perform some antics or other from time to time. Even in the poultry-yard we see the Cock showing off before his wives, strutting proudly hither and thither, crowing and flapping his wings. The Turkey is a more finished performer; as he dances about with tail widely spread and trailing wings he appears the very personification of conscious pride, though in this respect he is far surpassed by the Peacock. The way in which a Peacock approaches his lady-love is peculiar. Placing himself at some distance from her, he erects his train in a gorgeous fan and then, seizing a favourable opportunity,

COURTSHIP

rushes towards her *backwards* until, arrived within a foot or so, he suddenly whirls round and tries to overwhelm her with the glory of his plumage. His display, however, is not received with any obvious signs of admiration; on the contrary, the modest hen remains conspicuously indifferent, or appears so, even when the sudden transformation is emphasised by an ear-splitting scream. Both Peacock and Turkey produce music of the instrumental kind during their performance, the Turkey by scraping his quills along the ground, the Peacock by rattling his together, with a sound like the pattering of rain on leaves, as he turns towards his partner.

The courtship of Reinhardt's Ptarmigan (*Lagopus rupestris reinhardti*) of Greenland and Labrador is a very eccentric performance. Having discovered an eligible partner, he begins to run around her with tail spread and trailing wings; as his ardour increases he ruffles every feather of his body and, with outstretched neck and breast pressing upon the ground, thrusts himself along, uttering a curious growling sound. He writhes and twists his neck about in a wonderful manner, and at last in his excitement performs the most astonishing antics, leaping in the air with extraordinary vigour, and even rolling over and over.

Behaviour quite so violent as this is rare, but grotesque postures and contortions are seen in many species, especially in those which have some peculiar decoration to display. Such birds are immediately prompted to put themselves into the most showy attitude by the presence of the female or a rival, or even that of a stranger. Crests and plumes are raised, wings or tail spread, and various other means adopted to make any striking feature as conspicuous as possible. The result sometimes appears to us ridiculous in the extreme, but there is little doubt that the female is, as a rule, much impressed by the display of so much finery.

Occasionally, however, she seems to be singularly indifferent to the personal charms of her wooer, be they displayed never

COURTSHIP

so bravely. You may frequently observe this amongst domestic Pigeons. Watch a group of these birds picking up grain which has been scattered for them upon the ground; it is very likely that before long you will see a handsome cock-bird begin to pay court to a sober-looking hen. He puffs out his breast and throat to make himself look imposing and to display the glossy iridescent feathers to the best advantage; meanwhile he coos softly and bows time after time to the quiet little hen, running after her with quick steps and doing his very best to attract her attention. She for her part seems quite indifferent; she is far too busy picking up grains of food to trouble about the fussy courtier; she seems to show by her attitude that she thinks him a tiresome fellow, and cannot be bothered; and will he please go away? But he is far from being discouraged, and at last she runs forward a few steps to escape persecution; but he makes a flank movement, runs round in a little quarter-circle, and is once more in front of her, bowing, cooing, trailing his outspread tail along the ground, and using all his arts with undiminished zeal. It is most often in the spring and summer that one may see Pigeons behaving in this manner, but quite recently, in a London street, I observed the same little comedy being enacted amidst heavy rain in the middle of December. Neither the storm nor the season could affect the wooer's devotion.

A few years ago, when in Spain, in the neighbourhood of Seville, I was even more impressed by the efforts of a male bird to make himself attractive while the female remained absolutely unmoved. On a broad, open tract of cultivated land, less than half a mile from the road, a number of large birds were quietly feeding. With the aid of glasses I was able to make out that it was a small party of Bustards—the Great Bustard (*Otis tarda*), which used, long ago, to frequent the downs, wolds, and plains in England, but which has now been extinct as a native species for about three-quarters of a century. Perhaps it was never very common here, though there are records of it

COURTSHIP

having been at one time hunted with greyhounds on Newmarket Heath. Even in the sixteenth century, however, when Bustards were a favourite dish at great feasts, they were considered articles of special luxury and ranked in value with such birds as Swans and Cranes. But in Spain they are still fairly common, and great was my delight at having an opportunity of watching them in their wild state.

The party consisted of four females and a male. The hen Bustard is considerably smaller than the cock, which is a fine bird, between three and four feet in length from the tip of the bill to the end of the tail, and has a very stately and conspicuous appearance on the open country which he frequents. His colour is not very remarkable, pale grey and white predominating; but the back is beautifully barred with russet and black, and during the springtime a band of deep tawny brown sweeps down from either shoulder over the breast. His general aspect is made more striking by a beard of slender greyish-white feathers which spring out stiffly on either side of the chin. While I was observing the little group of birds, the male left off feeding and presently, after strutting to and fro for a short time, with head and tail both held proudly erect, he placed himself in the very remarkable attitude adopted by these birds when 'showing off.' The breast and upper part of the throat are puffed out to their utmost extent; at the same time the head is drawn far back and buried between the shoulders, while the tail is turned forwards flat upon the back, until head and tail almost meet between the wings. The wings themselves are then drooped from the shoulder, the ends of the long flight feathers are hitched up on the back across the tail, while the shorter feathers turn stiffly upwards and almost completely hide the head, the 'beard' alone being seen standing smartly up between them. The result of all these curious contortions is to display to the fullest extent the white feathers of the upper part of the wings and those under the tail.

In this strange posture my Bustard strutted up and down

COURTSHIP

before his wives for fully five minutes, but not one of them paid any attention to his performance or allowed herself to be diverted from her immediate occupation of feeding. At the end of that time he seemed suddenly to decide that perhaps they were right, after all, and that in any case it was not much use trying to show them what a very fine figure of a bird he was if none would admire him, for his head came up with a jerk, his wings were folded close to his body again, his breast gently subsided, and resuming his ordinary appearance he began once more quietly feeding with the others.

Bustards are very wary birds and it is exceedingly difficult to get quite near to them, but like many other wild creatures they appear to have a curious power of discrimination, so that while a sportsman carrying a gun may find it impossible to get within range of them, they do not so readily take alarm at the passage of an ordinary wayfarer.

A smaller kind of Bustard known as the Florikin (*Sypheotis bengalensis*), which is one of the most valued Game-birds in all parts of India, where it is frequently killed during a tiger-hunt and is occasionally taken by the help of the Falcon, is known to adopt somewhat unusual and remarkable tactics to attract a mate. The male bird rises, with hurried flapping of the wings, straight up into the air, pausing from time to time for a few seconds and then flying a little higher. While doing this he raises his crest, puffs out his neck, and makes a peculiar kind of humming noise. The performance is repeated several times until a hen obeys the summons and approaches from the thick grass, where they live apart. On her arrival he begins to entertain her by showing off in much the same manner as a Turkey-cock. The male Willow-Grouse in North America practises similar flights; his call, however, is often accepted as a challenge by some rival male, and fierce combats follow.

A very large number of birds puff out their feathers when courting in order to make themselves appear as big and important as possible; even the tiny Blue Titmouse swells himself

COURTSHIP

out to almost twice his usual size in the intervals of sailing from the top of one slender spray to another amongst the trees and bushes—a method of flight quite different from his ordinary movement from place to place—when dallying with his mate.

We have seen that it is not unusual for the female to receive the attentions of her wooer at first with apparent indifference, if not annoyance. In some cases she at length appears slowly to become aware of his existence, to display a sort of languid interest in his proceedings, to be willing to listen, without prejudice, to what he has to say, to spare a moment for a critical glance at his antics. Sometimes on hearing the sound of a performing male she may even deign to approach and stand by, hidden in the bushes, an interested spectator; she may utter little cries—perhaps her way of saying "Bravo!"—to incite him to further efforts, and may eventually, without reserve, seek his company.

In other cases, however, she is more coy and takes to flight—whether in earnest or not, who can say? Though her retreat be swift and energetic at first, it is often continued with little persistence, and it seems as if she wished to be overtaken.

Dr. Groos says: "The female Cuckoo answers the call of her mate with an alluring laugh that excites him to the utmost, but it is long before she gives herself up to him. A mad chase through the tree tops ensues, during which she constantly incites him with that mocking call, till the poor fellow is fairly driven crazy. The female Kingfisher often torments her devoted lover for half a day, coming and calling him, and then taking to flight. But she never lets him out of her sight the while, looking back as she flies and measuring her speed, and wheeling back when he suddenly gives up the pursuit. The Bower-bird leads her mate a chase up and down their skilfully built pleasure-house, and many other birds behave in a similar way. The male must exercise all his arts . . . before her reluctance is overcome. She leads him on from limb to limb,

COURTSHIP

from tree to tree, constantly eluding his eager pursuit until it seems that the tantalising change from allurement to resistance must include an element of mischievous playfulness."

There are birds, however, amongst which the hens are so far from being coy and retiring that they are actually the ones who make all the advances in courtship. In such cases we find that, contrary to what is the general rule amongst birds, the hen is the finer and better looking of the pair. As an example of these we will take the Phalaropes.

The Phalaropes are wading birds, and they nest in the Arctic regions, where they are extremely tame. In many species of waders—perhaps in all—the hen-bird is distinguished by her larger size and longer bill, but her superiority seldom extends to plumage. Among the Phalaropes, however, the females are not only larger, but brighter in colour than their partners, and in accordance with the general custom amongst birds in such cases they take the lead in courtship. Here is the interesting account of their proceedings given by Mr. E. W. Nelson, the well-known American field naturalist, who observed the Red-necked or Northern Phalarope (*Phalaropus hyperboreus*) in Alaska.

"As summer approaches on the Arctic shores and the coast of Bering Sea, the numberless pools, until now hidden under a snowy covering, become bordered or covered with water; the mud about their edges begins to soften, and through the water the melting ice at the bottom looks pale green. The Ducks and the Geese fill the air with their loud resounding cries, and the rapid wing-strokes of arriving and departing flocks add a heavy bass to the chorus which greets the opening of another glad season in the wilds of the cheerless north. Amid this loud-tongued multitude suddenly appears the graceful, fairy-like form of the Northern Phalarope. Perhaps, as the hunter sits by the border of a secluded pool still half covered with snow and ice, a pair of slight wings flit before him, and there, riding on the water, scarcely making a ripple, floats this charm-

COURTSHIP

ing and elegant bird. It glides hither and thither on the water, apparently drifted by its fancy, and skims about the pool like an autumn leaf wafted before the playful zephyrs on some embosomed lakelet in the forest. The delicate tints and slender, fragile form, combining grace of colour and outline with a peculiarly dainty elegance of motion, render this the most lovely and attractive bird amongst its handsome congeners.

". . . In the last few days of May and June they are on hand in full force and ready to set about the season's cares. Every pool now has from one to several pairs of these birds. . . . The female . . . is much more richly coloured than the male, and possesses all the 'rights' demanded by the most radical reformers. As the season comes on . . . the dull-coloured male moves about the pool apparently heedless of the surrounding females. Such stoical indifference usually appears too much for the feelings of some of the fair ones to bear. A female coyly glides close to him and bows her head in pretty submissiveness, but he turns away, pecks at a bit of food and moves off; she follows, and he quickens his speed, but in vain; he is her choice, and she proudly arches her neck, and in many circles passes and repasses close before the harassed bachelor. He turns his breast first to one side, then to the other, as though to escape, but there is his gentle wooer ever pressing her suit before him. Frequently he takes flight to another part of the pool, but all to no purpose. If with affected indifference he tries to feed, she swims along side by side, almost touching him, and at intervals rises on wing above him, and, poised a foot or two over his back, makes a half-dozen quick, sharp wing-strokes, producing a series of sharp, whistling noises in rapid succession.

"In the course of time it is said that water will wear the hardest rock, and it is certain that time and importunity have their full effect upon the male of this Phalarope, and soon all are comfortably married. . . . About June 1 the dry, rounded side of a little knoll, near some small pond, has four

COURTSHIP

dark, heavily marked eggs laid in a slight hollow, upon whatever lining the spot affords, or, more rarely, upon a few dry straws and grass-blades, brought and loosely laid together by the birds. Here the captive male is introduced to his new duties, and spends half his time on the eggs, while the female keeps about the pool close by. In due time the young are hatched and come forth, beautiful little balls of buff and brown."

With the more pugnacious birds, such as the Willow-Grouse, courtship and battle often go together; but many species are quite good-natured and peaceful in their rivalry—none more so, perhaps, than that common and conspicuous North American bird, the Golden-winged Woodpecker or Flicker (*Colaptes auratus*). This bird always seems to be on the best of terms with its neighbours, even when courting, and the sight of a couple of males paying their addresses to the same female is one of the most amusing comedies in bird-life. Their apparent shyness as they sidle up to her and hurriedly retire again, their queer little games of bo-peep as they slyly watch one another's advances from the shelter of some convenient limb of the tree, are exceedingly comic, and when at last the choice is made, the unsuccessful suitor retreats with dignity, taking his defeat quite philosophically, and no doubt enters into an equally friendly contest elsewhere.

Here we must make an end. This book tells of only a few of the wonderful things that we know about the lives of birds. In *The Romance of Bird Life*, from which these chapters are taken, you may read the story of their battles and piracy, their flight and swimming and diving; of their toilet, their social habits and strange friendships, their wisdom and folly; and you may learn also something of that sad tale of the persecution which has deprived the earth of some of its most interesting inhabitants.

END